MAKING BEAD FLOWERS AND BOUQUETS

by Virginia Nathanson

DOVER PUBLICATIONS, INC.
Mineola, New York

To my husband John and my two sons,
Rex and Brad, with love and appreciation
for their patience and understanding

Bibliographical Note

This Dover edition, first published in 1983 and reissued in 2002, is
an unabridged republication (by special arrangement with Nedda Anders
and Richard Anders) of the work originally published in 1967 by
Hearthside Press Incorporated, Publishers, N.Y., under the title *The Art of
Making Bead Flowers and Bouquets*. Of the original twelve color illustra-
tions, six appear in color on the covers and six appear in black-and-white
on pages 3–6.

Library of Congress Cataloging-in-Publication Data

Nathanson, Virginia.
    Making bead flowers and bouquets / Virginia Nathanson.
        p. cm.
    Reprint. Originally published under title: The art of making bead
flowers and bouquets. New York : Hearthside Press, 1967.
    Includes bibliographical references and index.
    ISBN 0-486-42246-1 (pbk.)
    1. Bead flowers. I. Nathanson, Virginia. Art of making bead flowers .
and bouquets. II. Title.

TT890.2 .N38 2002
745.58'2—dc21

                                                          2001055290

Manufactured in the United States of America
Dover Publications, Inc., 31 East 2nd Street, Mineola, N.Y. 11501

IV A SYMMETRICAL TRIANGLE IN BLUES AND WHITE . . . with fantasias, rose of Sharon, and daisies. V A HORIZONTAL BOUQUET . . . with delphinium, carnations, lilacs, anemones, and fuchsias.

IX THREE BOUQUETS . . . Chrysanthemums and gladiolus, with a cluster of rose of Sharon in a tall Lenox vase. Short sprigs of forsythia, day lilies, and sunflower leaves in a wicker basket. Morning glories and leaves in a brass cornucopia.

X MINIATURES . . . Tea roses and baby's breath, Shasta daisy, buds, irises, daffodils, and apple blossoms. In front are tea roses and two groupings of primroses.

XI POTTED PLANTS . . . Sunflower, orange tree, African violet, cabbage rose, hyacinth, tiger lily, geranium.

XII CHRISTMAS DECORATIONS . . . Silver tree, green tree, poinsettia plant, angel Christmas bells.

CONTENTS

ACKNOWLEDGMENTS

Not all of the arrangements shown in color*are the result of my own handiwork, and it is a great pleasure for me to give credit and thanks to the following students who were kind enough to lend me the bouquets which I designed but which they executed: Mrs. Harriet Bloom—morning glories in brass cornucopia; Mrs. Doris Cohn—arrangement of lilacs, carnations, and delphiniums; Mrs. Mary Demeter—marigolds; Mrs. Maxine Rudman—bowl of anemones and forsythia; Mrs. Arlene Seide—oriental poppies; Mrs. Jerry Unger—roses.

My special thanks also to Rae L. Goldson, author of *Contemporary Flower Arrangement* and *New Trends in Flower Arrangement* (also published by Hearthside Press). Her magic touch has been added to the arrangement of forsythia, fantasies, and daisies; pussy willows and daffodils; and the lilacs.

Also, I would like to thank Douglas Corry for his brilliant color photography, Pan-Ad for black and white photographs, and Julie Noonan for line drawings.

---

*Not all of these plates appear in color in the present edition. See p. 188 for full listing of all plates.

INTRODUCTION

The art of bead-flower making originated many centuries ago with the peasants of France and northern Italy who tended the vineyards in the wine country. Because these people were idle during the winter months, enterprising glass manufacturers gave them homework—the making of glass beads that were to embroider the magnificent ball gowns and jackets worn by the members of the French court. Imperfect beads were rejected, but rather than discard the beads, the thrifty peasants made them into beaded flowers which altar and choir boys carried in church processionals for Easter and Christmas services. Some flowers were arranged into bridal and altar bouquets, and others into funeral wreaths. In the latter part of the nineteenth century, clever interior decorators obtained some of these old wreaths and sprays, converting them into handsome wall sconces and lamps wired for this purpose.

Long before this time, however, beads had been a source of interest and fascination. The word itself is derived from "bede," Anglo-Saxon for prayer. Some forms of beads were looked upon as good-luck charms, some were used to repel evil spirits, still others were said to be imbued with the power to cure certain illnesses. Beads are among the oldest ornaments, having been used as far back as the ancient Egyptian civilization. The North American Indians who were noted for their heavily beaded articles of dress also used beads as "wampum."

What started as a personal hobby has become a full-time teaching career. Now with this book I hope to extend the pleasure and excitement of this craft to others. Once you have mastered the few necessary techniques, you can be your own designer, increasing or decreasing the size of the petals and other parts as you please. By creating these beaded flowers, you may even develop a keener sense of observation and really *see* your favorite flowers for the first time.

Flowers need not be small to be easy to make. Many large ones are just as simple, and so on the following pages there are flowers of all sizes. There is also a section on how to group them into attractive designs and color schemes.

Before you attempt your first project, read through the general instructions. Become familiar with the terminology used for various techniques. Then, as you perfect the basic technique, go on to make other flowers that use it. (You will find listed in the index all the articles which can be made by each of the techniques.) With practice, your flowers will become more professional. You can even become proficient enough to make a profitable part- or full-time business of bead flowers, because bouquets are always in demand by decorators and boutique shops. Since bead flowers are practically indestructible, they can also be sold by mail order. Beaded novelties are perfect "little gifts" for hostesses, bridge parties, and similar occasions; so they can be used for organization fund-raising. And if you enjoy teaching, perhaps you too can find a career in showing others how to make these sparkling, shimmering, magnificent little gems from beads.

I GENERAL INSTRUCTIONS

MATERIALS

Beads

Beads are small round objects pierced for stringing. They come in a variety of materials, sizes and shapes, but only glass beads are used for making flowers. There are transparent, lined and chalk (sometimes called opaque) beads that are perfectly round, others are faceted or cut and have a bit of glitter to them. There are bugle beads one-eighth to one-quarter of an inch long which produce special effects, but these are not generally used in making bead flowers. Beads can be bought strung, in bunches of 10 or 12 strings, or they can be bought packaged loose—the same quality is available either way. All beads are imported, as there are no bead factories in the United States and a wide range of colors is available. Here are our recommendations:

Perfectly round beads give the nicest effect

The best size is labeled 11°. (Size 12° is smaller and may be difficult to string onto the wire. Size 10° is larger and gives a less delicate effect.)

Transparent and opaque beads are best

Strung beads are easier to work with than loose ones, mainly because it is less time-consuming to transfer the strung beads from the thread to the wire

Quantities listed in this book are based on using bunches of beads that have 12 strings, each measuring about 20 inches in length.

Beads can be bought in hobby shops, through many craft catalogs, in department stores, etc.

Tools and other supplies

You will need

1. A small wire cutter. It can have either a side or top cutting surface. A small nail clipper will do an excellent job of cutting the spool wire, but it will not be sturdy enough for the stem wires.

2. A small, long-nose pair of jewelers pliers. This is optional, however, it does make the twisting of the wires easier.

3. Spool wire. For most petals, leaves, stamens, and sepals, you will need 28-gauge wire. Use 26-gauge wire for larger petals and leaves, as it is stiffer and a bit heavier than the 28-gauge, and it will make the larger units easier to execute. For lacing and assembling, you will need either 30- or 32-gauge wire.

4. Stem wires. 16-gauge wire to reinforce the larger flowers, and 18-gauge for the smaller ones.

5. Floral tape for assembling.

6. Modeling clay, the non-hardening kind, is the best material to use for potting your arrangements. Styrofoam will not hold the weight of most flowers.

7. Florist sheet moss. Available at most florist shops, it is an excellent covering for the clay. Small stone chips may be used instead of the moss, if desired.

8. Containers for the bouquets. Your own home will reveal many objects that can be used for this purpose. Inexpensive glass goblets and bowls which match or harmonize with the beads are an excellent choice, but these bead-flower arrangements are heirloom pieces, so do not hesitate to arrange them in your finest antique china (using care when stuffing it with modeling clay to avoid breakage).

METHODS

The first step is to string beads on wire. Strung beads are easier to transfer to wire than loose beads, but both methods are given below. After the beads are on wire, you can proceed to make the flowers, but read through and understand the methods given in this chapter. Become familiar with the terminology. Try a few methods. A good starting flower is the Star Daisy, which has leaves and petals using pointed tops and round bottoms. Practice the leaves first. If your points are not too perfect, they will go unnoticed. By the time you have made fifteen or twenty of them, the points will be as they should be. Then, making the flower petals will seem easy. Don't worry if you suddenly develop ten thumbs; all beginners do. With practice, you can go on to make beautiful bouquets. Some of the plates show flower arrangements made by pupils, all of whom began with those ten thumbs.

One word of caution, keep finished flower parts separated from bunches of beads by putting them in envelopes or plastic bags. The wires of the units can become entangled in the strands of beads and cause the strings to become loose.

Should you spill beads, the best way to pick them up is to moisten the end of a finger, press the finger into the beads, then put the beads onto the wire, one at a time.

After the beads are strung on wire, various techniques are used in making flowers and leaves. Once you understand these general techniques, you can make every flower in the book, varying the bead count or measurement according to the directions given. The techniques, all described in this chapter and illustrated with step-by-step drawings are: Basic (Basic Loop, Round Petal, Pointed Petal and Leaf) Continuous Single Loops, Continuous Wraparound Loops, Continuous Loopbacks, Continuous Crossover Loops, Shading of Petals, Lacing, Beaded Stems, and Assembly and Use of Floral Tape.

Stringing beads on wire

Open the spool of wire. If you are working with a wooden spool, put a thumb tack in the top so that you can wrap the wire around it. This will prevent the wire from spiraling off the spool. Cut the open end of the wire on the bias (at an angle) to achieve a good point; the beads will go onto the wire much easier. If you are working with loose beads, spill a fair amount into a small saucer or cup, dip the open end of the spool wire into the beads, catching the beads on the wire. Repeat until the required number of beads are strung. If you are working with strung beads, gently ease out one end of a strand of beads from the bunch. Insert the open end of the spool wire into the

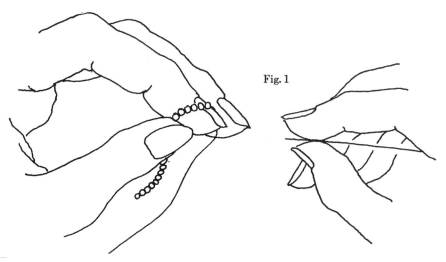

Fig. 1

beads, then remove the thread from the beads that are already on the wire. *Fig. 1.*

It's not necessary to take too many beads at a time. An inch or so is sufficient. You'll find that with a little practice, the stringing will go very quickly. When one-half strand of beads has been transferred to the spool of wire, knot the open end of the string of beads, making the knot large enough to prevent beads from slipping off. Gently remove the opposite end of the strand from the bunch, and continue transferring the remaining beads onto the wire, from the open end of the strand. This procedure will prevent spillage of beads. It is seldom necessary to string more than 2 or 3 strands at a time.

Should you run out of beads before finishing a petal or leaf, measure enough wire by going around the petal or leaf with bare wire, for the required number of rows, allow 3 or 4 inches of extra wire, and, at this point, cut the wire from the spool. Feed onto the open end of wire the amount of beads required to finish the petal or leaf. Crimp the open end of the wire after putting on the amount of beads needed, so that the beads won't slip off, then continue making the unit.

Unless otherwise specified

> Never work with a cut piece of wire
>
> Always work directly from the spool
>
> Always complete each petal or leaf before cutting the wire from the spool
>
> Crimp the open end of the spool wire after the required number of beads have been strung on the spool

Basic Technique

This technique is the one which is used most often for individual leaves and petals. The word "Basic:", when followed by a number, tells you how many beads or inches of string beads are to be put on the center wire, around which the remaining beads are wrapped.

Making the basic loop. Crimp the open end of the wire, move the required number of beads (the basic count) to within 4″ of the crimped end of the wire. If you hold your work from underneath, your hands won't hide your work. Place your left thumb and forefinger under the wire and to the right of the basic beads. Place your right thumb and forefinger under the wire and to the left of the remaining beads on the spool of wire. *Fig. 2.*

Keep the spool of wire to the right. Have at least 5″ of bare wire between your forefingers. Bring your forefingers together, as in

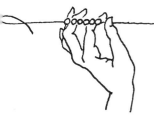

Fig. 2

Fig. 3 and transfer the basic beads to your right thumb and fore-finger. With your left hand, twist together the loop of wire that is under your right thumb and forefinger. Twist 4 or 5 times very tightly at the bottom of the basic beads. Starting on the left side of the basic beads, bring the beaded wire up the left side of the basic beads, wrap bare beading wire once around the bare wire at the top of the basic beads—where the single wire is—then come down the right side of the basic beads with beads, and wrap bare beading wire once around the loop wires at the base of the basic beads. Always cross the bare beading wire across the front, to the back, and around to the front again. *Fig. 4.*

Continue wrapping the strung beads around the basic beads until you have the number of rows called for in your pattern. Keep the rows of beads and the beads themselves close together, and wrap the wires, top and bottom, tightly. The less wire you have showing, the more solid effect you will get. Your units will be firmer, too. Keep the basic wire as straight through the center as possible as you work. Keep the right side of your petals and leaves facing you as you wrap. After the first few rows have been made, the wrong side will be obvious to you, as more wire shows on the wrong side. To determine the number of rows, count the rows across the center, in-

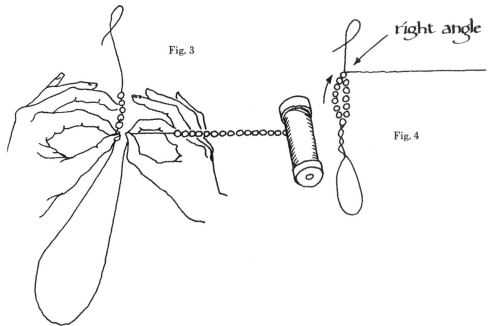

Fig. 3

right angle

Fig. 4

cluding the basic row in your count. The single wire is always con-
sidered the top of the petal or leaf, and the loop is the bottom. Always
finish at the bottom. This will give you an odd number of rows. There
are only a few patterns that call for an even number of rows, in which
instance you will finish your work at the top of the unit, where the
single wire is.

Round Petals. Round petals are usually easier for the beginner to
make, so try a round one, making a basic of 5 beads with 7 rows. As
you wrap the bare beading wire around the top and bottom of the
basic beads, keep the wire close to the row of beads that precedes it.
Each pattern has been figured mathematically to achieve the proper
dimension, therefore don't create a roundness by bowing out the rows
of beads. Keep each new row of beads close to the one next to it. As
you make the first wrap at the top of the basic beads, cross in front
of the top basic wire, so that the spool wire is horizontal and at right
angles to the top basic wire. Wrap the spool wire completely around
the top wire, stopping at a right angle position. *Fig. 4.* Push beads to
the top of the basic beads. Turn the petal counter-clockwise with the
left hand (so that the loop is at the top). Wrap bare wire around the
basic loop—at a right angle—just as you did at the top around the
single wire. *Fig. 5.* Turn your work counter clockwise again, and
repeat, wrapping at the top and at the bottom until the 7 rows have
been completed.

  As each petal and leaf is finished, cut the top basic wire ¼" from
the top, and bend the ¼" of wire down the back of the unit. Tuck it
in neatly. Allow 4" of bare spool wire at the bottom of the petal or

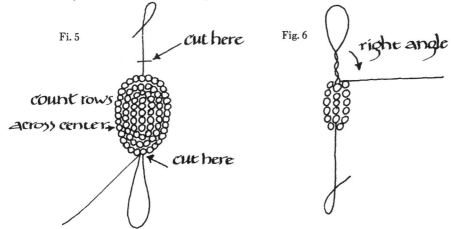

Fi. 5   cut here   Fig. 6   right angle

count rows
across center

cut here

leaf, and cut the unit free from the spool of wire. Cut open the basic loop at the base of the petal, then twist the two remaining wires together. *Fig. 6.*

Pointed petals and leaves. Some petals and leaves have pointed tops and round bottoms, others have round tops and pointed bottoms. Wherever the point, the basic method for making them is the same, except for one slight change. To create a point, go 2 beads beyond the basic beads before wrapping around the wires, and change the angle of the spool wire to a 45° angle in relation to the basic wire. Push the beads into the point, and shape it by squeezing the rows of beads together, then flattening the rows so that they do not overlap one another. See *Fig. 7* for a pointed top and *Fig. 8* for a pointed bottom.

Once the point is started, it must be kept, or the effect is lost, so repeat the procedure each time you work up to the point. For a pointed bottom, start the point at the end of the third row. For a pointed top, start the point at the end of the second row.

Continuous Single Loops

Many flowers are made with continuous loops, each loop worked close to the preceding one. Bells of Ireland, Canterbury Bells, Carna-

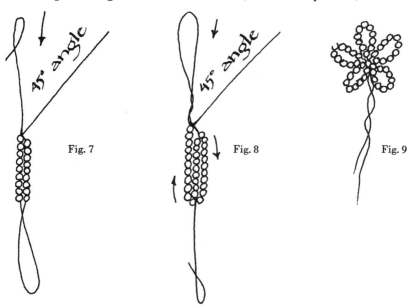

Fig. 7   Fig. 8   Fig. 9

tions, Daffodil crowns, and Marigolds are just a few that are made with the loop method. Several flowers use continuous loops for centers, too. To make small loop units for centers, the number of beads used for each loop are counted. For large flower units, the beads are measured. This enables you to work faster and more accurately.

To make a small center consisting of five 10-bead loops, put a few inches of beads onto the spool wire, crimp the open end of the wire, and move 10 beads to within 4″ of the crimped end of the wire. Make a loop of these 10 beads by twisting the wire close to the base of the loop. Twist the wires tightly together, twice. Close to the base of the first loop, form another ten-bead loop, and give the 10 beads at least one full twist. It makes no difference whether the twist is toward you or away from you. Just be consistent with your direction. Most right-handed people make each new loop to the left of the preceding one, but if it is easier for you to work from left to right, do so, as the end result will be the same. By turning the loops of beads for one full twist, you will be crossing the wires at the base of the loops. Close to the base of the second loop, form a third loop with 10 beads, and give this loop a full twist. Make the 4th and 5th loops in the same way. After the 5th loop has been twisted, allow 4″ of bare wire, and cut the wire from the spool. Twist the 2 wires under the loops to form a stem, and you have completed a center. *Fig. 9.*

Continuous Wraparound Loops

Wraparound petals and leaves are made the same way as the single loops, except that each small loop of beads is encircled with beads around the outside edge, giving it a double row of beads. Let's make the same center as before, but wrap around each loop with beads as we wire. String more beads, crimp the open end of the spool wire, and move 10 beads to within 4″ of the crimped end of the wire. Make a loop of the 10 beads, then wrap around the outside of this loop of beads with the beaded wire. Wrap bare spool wire around the beginning wire at the base of the wrapped loop of beads. Next to this, but not quite as close as for making single loops, make another 10-bead loop. Give the loop of beads one full twist, then encircle it with beads. Wrap the bare beading wire around the base of the second loop. Execute the 3rd, 4th, and 5th loops in the same manner, taking care to wrap bare bead wire around the base of each petal after the loop has been encircled with beads. Allow 4″ of bare spool wire at the completion of the last petal, and cut the wire from the spool. *Fig. 10.* The butterfly body, anemone centers, and the geranium flowers are made with continuous wraparound loops.

Continuous Loopbacks

There are several patterns in which this method is used. It occurs first in the Anemone calyx, and the directions are given in detail with that flower. Just be certain that the bead wire is continuous so that the complex calyx is done on one length of wire. This method is also used in making leaves for rose of sharon, shasta daisy, dahlia and chrysanthemum. The technique is the same in every case, but the first unit measurement varies.

Continuous Crossover Loops

Flowers made with the crossover method are basically the same as the continuous single loop, except that each loop has beading either up the front and down the back (for a four-row crossover) or beading up the front and bare wire down the back (for a three-row crossover). The initial loops should be measured for uniformity in size.

String at least 24″ of beads, crimp the open end of the wire, and move 1½″ of beads to within 4″ of the crimped end of the wire. Form the 1½″ of beads into a *narrow* loop, and tightly twist the wires at the base of the loop twice. Bring the beaded wire up the front of the narrowed loop, using just enough beads to fill in the center of the loop. Push the extra beads away, so that the bare wire goes in between the beads at the top of the loop. Bring bare bead wire down the back of the loop, flatten the petal in the middle so that all three rows are visible. Wrap bare bead wire around the single wire at the base of the petal. You have just made one three-row crossover petal. Close to the base of the first petal, form a loop with another 1½″ of beads, give the loop of beads one full twist, narrow the loop, bead up the front of the loop, bring bare bead wire down the back, and wrap bare bead wire around the base of the second petal. Repeat for 5 more petals. Allow 4″ of bare bead wire at the completion of the 7th petal, and cut the wire from the spool. Twist the two wires together to form a stem. *Fig. 11.* Make a center for this flower in a contrast color, by using the wraparound method. Make a loop of 8 beads. Wrap around this loop with beads, cut the wire from the spool, twist the two wires together, and set the stamen flat, and in the center of the crossover flower. Measurements for this little crossover daisy can be decreased or increased as you desire. Change the original loop measurement to 2″, bead up the front and down the back for each petal, and make 9 or 10 petals instead of 7 as for the smaller one. Increase the count of the stamen to two wraparounds instead of only one, and you have a larger stamen for a larger daisy. The continuous crossover loops are used to create the Chrysanthemum, Daisy, Lilac, and Wheat.

Shading of Petals

Should you wish to shade any of your petals, it is necessary to leave enough bare wire on the petal to completely finish it, as contrast colors must be fed onto the open end of the wire. For example, make a round petal with a 5-bead basic and 7 rows. Work the 5 basic beads and the first 5 rows in the first color. Measure enough bare wire to go once more around the petal, measure another 4″ of bare wire

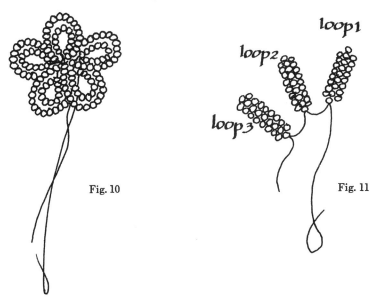

Fig. 10

loop1

loop2

loop3

Fig. 11

and cut the wire from the spool. Feed onto this open end of the wire at the base of the petal enough beads in a contrast second color to work rows 6 and 7. Tipping a petal can be done in the same way. Merely change the color of the beads on the top half of the last two rows, finishing off with the original color on the bottom half of the last row. Very attractive effects can be achieved with edging and tippings. *Figs. 12 and 13.*

Lacing

Lacing is the method used for reinforcing large petals and leaves. One form laces every row together, and the other form skip laces. Lacing is also used to join petals together in a continuous row, as is done on the tulip petals.

To reinforce a single petal or leaf, always start in the middle of the unit. Cut a piece of 30- or 32-gauge assembly wire approximately three times the width of the unit to be laced. Straddle the middle of the basic row with the assembly wire. Make sure the right side of your work is facing up, unless you are specifically instructed to do otherwise. Cross the assembly wires over one another, on the wrong side of the unit. You will be back-stitching from the center row to the

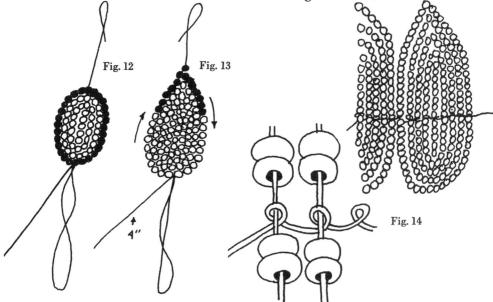

Fig. 12   Fig. 13

4"

Fig. 14

outside row, working one side of the unit at a time. Keep the top of
the unit to the left. Using the piece of assembly wire that is pointing
away from you, bring it under the row of beads next to the basic
row (the third row), up between the 3rd and 5th rows, across the top
of the 3rd row, and down in front of the 3rd row. Bring the wire
under the 3rd and 5th rows, up in back of the 5th row, down in front
of the 5th row, under the 5th and 7th rows, up in back of the 7th
row, down in front of the 7th row, etc. until the outer row has been
reached. Lace the outer row also—going around the outer row twice
to secure the wire. Clip the excess wire away, very close to the beads.
Reverse your work so that the bottom of the unit is to the left, still
right side up, and lace the other side of the unit in the same way,
bringing the other piece of wire under row 2, up behind row 2, down
in front of row 2, under rows 2 and 4, up behind row 4, over the top
of row 4, down in front of row 4, under rows 4 and 6, up behind
row 6, over the top of row 6, down in front of row 6, under rows 6
and 8 etc. until all of the remaining rows have been laced. Wrap
twice around the last row and clip away the excess lacing wire close
to the beads. On some very large petals, such as the largest petals on
the rose and the cabbage rose, you can bypass 6 or 7 rows on each
side of the basic row, then start your lacing to the outside rows.

When joining petals, one to the other—as for tulips—use approximately 15″ of assembly wire. Start in the middle of the first petal,
straddling the basic row. Leave 3″ of the assembly wire toward you,
and the remaining long piece of wire away from you. Cross the wires
over in the back, then with the long piece of wire, lace to the outside
row of the first petal, wrapping around the last row only once. Place
the second petal close to the first one, making sure that the tops of
the petals are even. Bring the lacing wire under, over and down in
front of the first row of the second petal. Continue lacing all the way
across the center of the second petal, then add the third petal and
lace it across the center. Repeat until the required number of petals
have been laced together. Turn your work around, still right side up,
and finish lacing the other half of the first petal, using the short piece
of wire. Try to keep the lacing in as straight a line as possible.
Fig. 14.

Skip-lacing is used for loop units as in Canterbury Bells, Bells of Ireland, Carnation calyx, Daffodil crown, Orchid throat, etc. For skip-lacing, cut a piece of assembly wire approximately 4 times the width of the unit to be laced. Insert one end of the wire into the first loop, leaving about 2" of wire extending through the loop. Wrap the longer piece of wire completely around the first loop, bring the wire under loops 1 and 2, over the top of loop 2. Pull the wire toward you. This will draw loop 2 close to loop 1. Bring the wire down between loops 1 and 2, under loops 2 and 3, up between loops 3 and 4, over the front of loop 3—pull the wire toward you, then bring the wire down between loops 2 and 3. Continue under loops 3 and 4, up between loops 4 and 5, over the front of loop 4, down between loops 3 and 4, under loops 4 and 5, up between loops 5 and 6, etc. until all loops have been wrapped around with the assembly wire. *Fig. 15.*

Beaded Stems

There are two ways in which flower stems may be beaded. The large flowers should be wrapped with small beads. However most medium size and small flower stems can be beaded by using large green stem beads.

For wrapped beaded stems, string the small regular green beads on 30- or 32-gauge wire. String at least three strands of beads, as most stems will require that much. After stringing the beads on the wire, wrap the open end of the spool wire around the stem at the base of

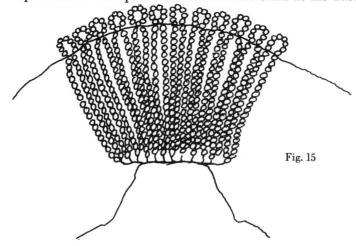

Fig. 15

the flower. Wrap it tightly, three or four times. Push beads up to the stem, and wrap around the stem with beads. Continue wrapping until the desired length has been achieved. Push beads away from the stem (toward the spool), and wrap bare spool wire around the stem three or four times. Cut the wire from the spool, and cover the bare wire with tape.

When using large green stem beads, use 19-gauge wire for the stem of the flower. Always hook the 19-gauge wire into the wires at the base of the flower to be stemmed. The hook need not be longer than ½ to ¾ of an inch. Secure the hook by covering the wires with one width of tape, wrapping the tape around twice. *Fig. 16.* After placing the large stem beads onto the 19-gauge stem wire to the desired length, tape the remaining stem wire, but include the last two stem beads in the taping. This will prevent the stem beads from slipping and the stem of the flower from turning.

Assembly and use of floral tape

All bare wires at the base of the leaves, and all flower stems (not individual petals) should be covered with floral tape before adding leaves and flowers to stems. If a heavy stem wire is to be used to give the flower stems more strength, cover this, too. Tear 15 or 20 inches of tape from its roll, and stretch it as far as possible. Always stretch the tape before using. It will be thinner, and stems will be slimmer. The tape is slightly adhesive and it has no right or wrong side. Attach the tape to the base of the flower stems and leaf stems and wrap downward at a bias angle. Press as you wrap. Cover heavy stem wires in the same manner. Should you need more tape before the wires are covered, simply add another piece of tape to where you left off, and continue. Add leaves to flower stems with more tape.

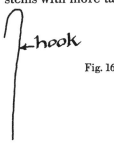

hook

Fig. 16

II FLOWERS AND LEAVES

Flower—2½″ wide; leaf—3″ long,
¾″ wide. See also Plate V, VIII.

ANEMONE OR WINDFLOWER

ANEMONE PULSATILLA is one of the most popular of all flowers for the advanced student. It is quite a challenge because it involves 5 different techniques. The natural hues are vibrant jewel tones of sapphire, ruby, amethyst, topaz, and white. These colors in an "anemone only" arrangement (which is the handsomest way to use them) fit any room, no matter what its décor.

Materials

Petals, ½ bunch for each flower
Centers, ½ strand for Unit 1, 1½ strands for Unit 2
Calyx, ½ strand for each
Leaves, ½ strand for each

Petals

BASIC: 4 beads, round tops, very pointed bottoms, 11 rows.
   Make 6 for each flower.

Centers (Beehive)

Unit 1.   BASIC: 2 beads, 10 rows. Make 1 for each flower in black.
   Because this unit calls for 10 rows, you will finish it at the top, at the single basic wire. Work this count through the fourth row, then bend the basic wire and the bottom basic loop downward. Shorten the following rows, so that you will use fewer beads than if you were making a flat disc. The aim is to create a mounded cap. *Fig. 17.*

Unit 2. Three inches from the open end of the spool wire, make a loop of 10 beads. Wrap twice around this loop with beads. Repeat until you have six 10-bead loops, each one wrapped twice with beads. Make 1 for each flower. *See Fig. 10.*

Calyx

The count is one 1″ loop of beads plus 4 continuous loopbacks (2 on each side of the 1″ loop).Make 3 for each flower.

Make a loop of 1″ of green beads. Keep the loop oval in shape. Make the first loopback on the left side of the original loop. Follow the directions of the wires in the diagram. After shaping the second loop, cross the spool wire over the front of the beginning wire at the base of the first loop, swing the wire to the back, and then forward and in between the original loop and the first loopback. Form the second loopback to the right of the original loop, but wrap the beading wire completely around the beginning wire. Form the third loopback to the left side again, cross the beading wire over the front of the beginning wire, swing the wire to the back, and then forward in between the first loopback and the one you are working on. Form the fourth loopback on the right side of your work, and wrap the beading wire completely around the beginning wire, then twist the 2 wires together. *Fig. 18.*

Leaves

Three inches from the open end of the spool wire, make loop with 1¼″ of beads. Twist the wires at the base of the loop twice. Push 9 beads to the base of the loop, and adjoining this, measure another 1¼″ of beads. Make another loop of 1¼″ of beads and twist the wires together twice. Continue in this manner until you have 9 loops of

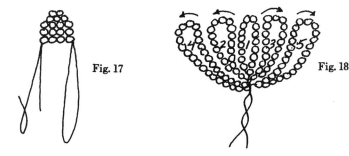

Fig. 17   Fig. 18

1¼" of beads separated by 9 beads. *Fig. 19.* Twist together the end wires. This will fold the string in half. *Fig. 20.* Make a half twist *(Fig. 21)* between each pair of loops, and slant the loops upward. Tape the stems. Make 3 for each flower.

Assembly of Flower

Combine the 2 center units by placing the black mound in the center of the wraparound unit. Twist the 2 sets of wires together, tape them, and cut off all but 1" of wire.

For an *unbeaded stem,* cut a piece of 16-gauge wire to the desired length and tape it. Tape the combined center units to the top of the heavy stem wire. Attach a 20" piece of assembly wire to the base of the combined center units. Wrap the wire tightly. With the assembly wire, add all 6 of the flower petals, one at a time, wrapping tightly with each addition. Add the calyx in the same way, one at a time. Add the petals right side up and the calyx wrong side up. Cut off the excess assembly wire, and thin out the remaining wires from the other units. Cover the wires with tape. Tape on the 3 leaves, one at a time, about 4" or 5" below the base of the flower. Tape all 3 leaves at the same level around the stem.

For *beaded stems,* use the large green stem beads, cut a piece of 19-gauge wire to the desired length, and bend ¾" of the wire at one end to form a hook. Catch this hook into the base wires of the flower. Pinch the hook closed with a plier and tape for 1" to secure. Cut away the petal and calyx wires at the base of the taping. String a strand of small green beads onto assembly wire, and wrap the taped part of the stem with the green beads. When the tape is covered, push away the excess beads on the spool and wrap assembly wire around the bare stem wire, very tightly, 3 or 4 times. Cut off the assembly wire close to the 19-gauge stem wire. Now slip onto the stem wire about 3 or 4 inches of large stem beads. Tape the remaining stem wire and include the last 2 stem beads as you tape. This will hold the stem more firmly. Tape 3 leaves to the base of the beaded stem.

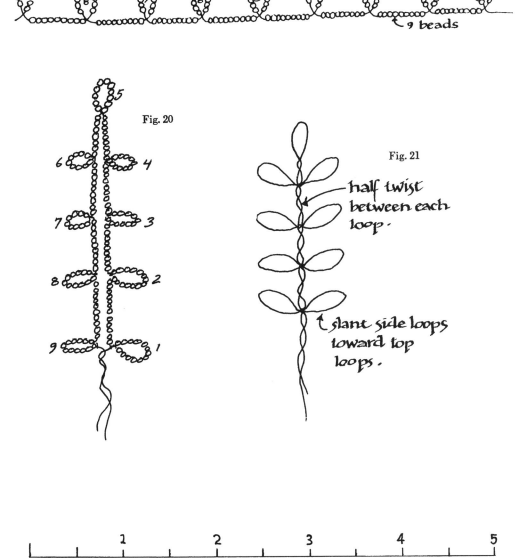

Fig. 19

¼" of beads

9 beads

Fig. 20

Fig. 21

half twist
between each
loop.

slant side loops
toward top
loops.

BABY'S BREATH
See Plate VIII, X.

GYPSOPHILA PANICULATA is a dainty accent for roses, sweet peas, and carnations, lovely in any of the miniature bouquets. The units are made the same for both large and small arrangements. For large arrangements, the little units are combined. Use 5 of them mounted on a piece of 16- or 18-gauge wire. For the miniature, use singly and mount on a short piece of 18-gauge wire.

Materials

Three inches of white beads for each unit
26- or 28-gauge wire (brass, green, or silver)

Twig

String approximately 3" of beads and crimp the end of the wire. Push 6 or 7 beads to within 5" of the crimped end of the wire, and make a loop of the beads. If you turn the loop instead of the wires, it will be easier for you to make the loop tight. Twist the 2 wires together for ½". On the left side of the twisted wires, ½" out, make another loop of 6 or 7 beads, and twist the wires together to where the wires are twisted below the first loop, *Fig. 22.* Directly opposite the second loop, and to the right of the first one, make a third loop of 6 or 7 beads. Twist together the 2 wires at the base of the 3rd loop until you have twisted back to the untwisted wire (A). Twist more wire together at the base of the first unit of 3 loops for 1". Make another loop of 6 or 7 beads, 1" to the left of the first unit of 3 loops. Twist the wires at the base of this loop for ½"; make another loop of beads to the left—½" out—and twist the wires together to B. Make a third loop of beads directly opposite, and to the right of the second loop, ½" out. Twist the wires back to B. Twist the 2 bare wires together for 1". Repeat in the same manner another unit of three 7-bead loops on the right side of the first 2 units, then twist the 2 wires together. Cover the 2 wires with tape and they are ready to either be combined for a large spray and stemmed, or used individually and stemmed. *Fig. 23.*

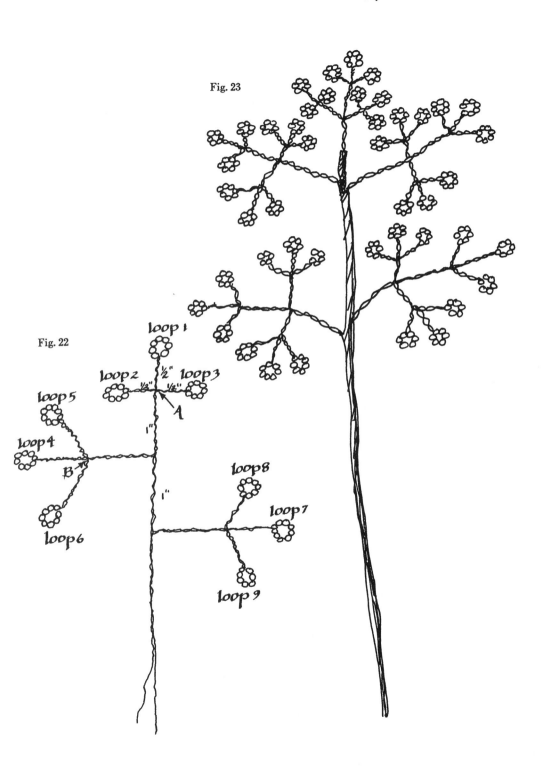

Fig. 23

Fig. 22

loop 1

loop 2 ½" loop 3

½" ½"

A

loop 5

1"

loop 4

B

loop 8

1"

loop 7

loop 6

loop 9

Flower—2½" high,
2¼" wide, 10" stem.

BEARDED IRIS

The iris can be made in one solid color with a contrast color for the beard and stamen, or it can be made in two colors. It has six petals in all—3 up petals and 3 down petals. One up petal has the stamen attached to it, and all 3 down petals have beards attached to them. The 3 up petals can be made in 1 color—pale lavender, for example—and the 3 down petals can be made in a deeper tone—purple—and the beards can be executed in pale lavender, or a pale yellow can be used for both stamen and beard.

Materials

Petals, 1 strand beads for one petal
Leaves, 2¼ strands for 1 leaf
Beard and Stamen, 1 strand in a contrast color
Wire, 26- or 28-gauge for all parts; 16-gauge wire for stems

Petals

BASIC: 7 beads, round tops, very pointed bottoms, 11 rows. Make 6.

Cut off the top basic wire on the 3 up petals. Do *not* cut them off on the 3 down petals. Cut open the basic loop at the base of all petals. On 2 up petals, cut off all but 2" of the bottom wires. On 1 up petal, leave 10" of spool wire before cutting the petal from the spool. On all 3 down petals, leave 10" of spool before cutting the petals from the spool wire. The extra 10" of wire are going to be used to create the stamen on 1 up petal and the beards on the 3 down petals. Let's make the stamen first. Onto the extra 10″ of wire, feed enough beads of a contrast color to form a narrow loop that reaches from the bottom of the petal to the top of the basic row. Make the loop on the wrong side of the petal. Twist the bottom wires together, and give the loop two half twists. To create the beard, feed onto the 10″ of wire enough beads of a contrast color to make a narrow loop that reaches from the bottom of the petal to the top of the petal, and back down to the bottom of the petal. Set this loop on the *right* side of the petal. Twist the bottom wires together. Give the narrow loop 2 half twists. Anchor this loop by bringing the top basic wire forward, through the top of the loop, and out the back of the petal. As you push the wire out the back of the petal, put the wire between the last row and the next to last row of the petal. Pull the wire tightly and cut it off close to the petal.

Assembly of Flowers

Cup the 3 up petals, wrong sides in, and twist the wires together. Tape the wires. Tape a 9 or 10″ piece of 16-gauge wire, and tape it to the base of the three up petals. Attach a 15″ piece of assembly wire to the base of the 3 up petals. Wrap it tightly, 3 or 4 times. Separate the petals, slightly. Add the 3 down petals, one at a time, right side up, in between the 3 up petals. When all petals have been added, wrap the asembly wire around the stem 3 or 4 times more, then cut off the excess. Cover the wires with tape. Reshape the up petals, curve the down petals down, and bend the head of the flowers forward.

Leaves

BASIC: 4″, pointed tops, round bottoms, 7 rows. Make 2 for each flower.

Cut open the basic loop at the bottom of the loop. Twist the wires together, and tape them. Five-and-a-half inches below the base of the flower, tape on 2 leaves, 1 on the left and 1 on the right.

Spray—16″ high; small flower— 1½″ wide;
medium flower—2″ wide; large flower—2½″ wide.

BELLS OF IRELAND

When creating Bells of Ireland (MOLUCELLA LAEVIS), I took liber-
ties with size. My bells are much larger than they grow naturally, but
as beaded flowers I think they are more effective in an increased
scale. You may reduce them in size, if you wish, by shortening the
count on all units by ½ to ⅓ of an inch, and by making fewer loops
(1 or 2). The bells grow naturally from pale green in the small size
to deep green in the larger ones. Making them this color will enable
you to use them as greenery fill-ins in any arrangement. However, by
executing them in three shades of pink, lavender, orange, red,
blue, or yellow, they become soft, lacy flowers that will add grace
and line to any arrangement that tends to be rather stiff and formal.
This spray of bells, when finished, should measure approximately
10″ in length, because there are 2 bells in each size—2 small, 2
medium, and 2 large. Should you wish to make a shorter spray,
make one bell in each size.

Bells

Small. Make 14 continuous single loops, measuring 2″ of beads for
each loop. Leave 2″ of wire for stem. Make 2 in the palest color.
Medium. Make 18 continuous single loops, measuring 2½″ of beads
for each loop. Leave 2″ of wire for stem. Make 2 in medium color.

Large. Make 22 continuous single loops, measuring 3" of beads for each loop. Make 2 in deepest color. Keep all loops narrow and very close together at the bottom by creating each new loop directly next to the previous ones. Each bell must be skip-laced ⅓ of the way up from the bottom. *Fig. 24.* Do this before closing them. Use the same method as for the Daffodil crowns, and the Canterbury Bells.

Stamens

Unit 1. Make 3 continuous single loops using 12 beads for each loop. Twist the wires together, twice, at the base of the loops. Onto each wire, string 1" of green beads. Twist the 2 wires together at the base of the green beads. *Fig. 25.* Make 1 in a contrasting color, usually yellow, for each flower.

Unit 2. (Same color as Unit 1) Make 6 continuous single loops, using 10 beads for each loop. Combine Unit 1 and Unit 2 by setting Unit 2 at the bottom of the green beads of Unit 1. Twist both sets of wires together. *Fig. 26.* Make 1 for each flower.

Calyx

Make 6 continuous single loops using 1" of beads for each loop. Make 1 in green for each flower.

Fig. 25

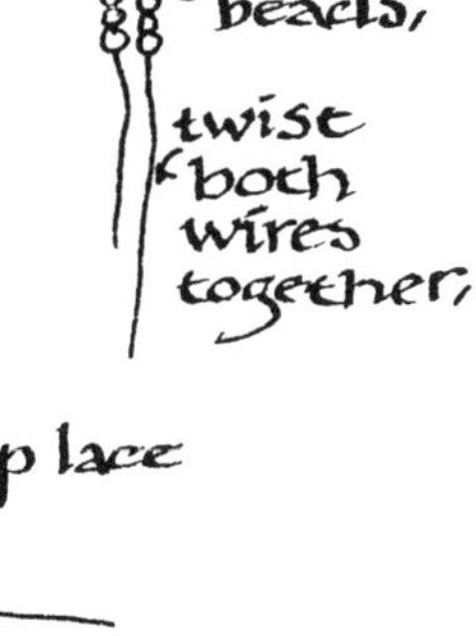

1" of green beads, twist both wires together,

skip lace

Fig. 26

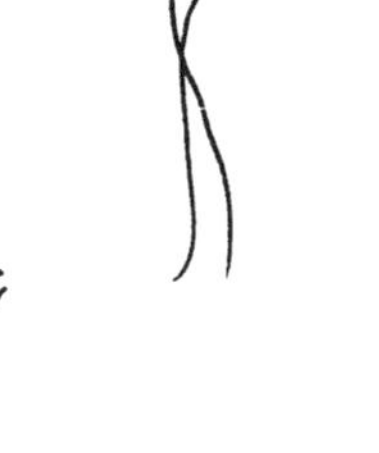

Fig. 24

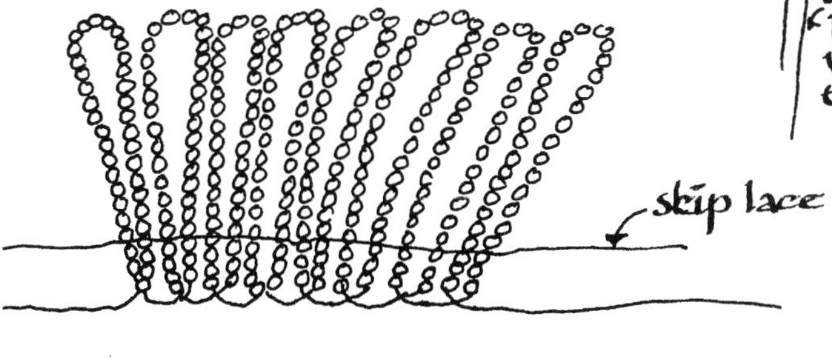

Assembly of Bells

After skip-lacing all of the bells, fold them, right side in, twist the lacing wires together, and cut off all but ¼" of the wire. Tuck the twisted wire in between the rows of beads. Twist the bell wires together only once or twice—just enough to keep the bell closd. Insert the combined Units 1 and 2 of the stamen into the bells so that the six 10-bead loops fill the opening at the bottom of the bell. Combine all wires at the bottom of the bell and twist them together to form a stem. Add a calyx to the bottom of each bell, and twist the calyx wires to the stem wires of the bell. Cover the combined wires with tape.

Leaves

The leaves are made with continuous single loops. However, the loops are separated by beads. String a few strands of green beads, and crimp the end of the wire. Move 1" of beads to within 3" of the crimped end of the wire. Make a loop with this 1" of beads, twisting the wires together, twice, tightly at the base of the loop. Count off 6 beads and move them close to the base of the loop. Measure another 1" of beads, make a loop of it close to the opposite end of the 6 beads, and continue until you have 7 loops, each one separated by 6 beads. *Fig. 27.* When you have finished the seventh loop, allow 3" of wire, and cut the wire from the spool. Onto each open end of wire put 1" of green beads, and twist the bottom wires together so that these beads are close to the base of loops 1 and 7. This will actually fold your string of loops in half. *Fig. 27.* Narrow the 7 loops by pinching them together. Give the unit a half twist in between each pair of loops. Put a sharp outward bend in the middle of each loop so that the green leaf resembles *Fig. 28.* Tape the stem wires. Make 8 in green.

Assembly of Spray

Tape a 12" piece of 16-gauge wire, attach a piece of tape to the top of the wire, and tape on a leaf, a flower, a leaf, a flower, etc., until all flowers and leaves have been added. Allow approximately ¾" of space between each leaf and flower. Tape the leaves flush to the master stem—no leaf stem showing—but allow 2" to 2½" of stem on the bells so that they can hang down, gracefully. When all leaves and flowers have been taped to the master stem, give the master stem a gentle "S" curve.

Fig. 27

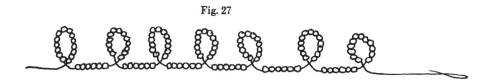

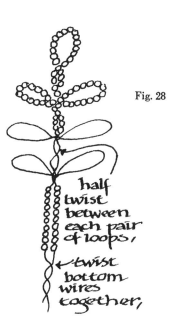

Fig. 28

half twist between each pair of loops;

twist bottom wires together;

1   2   3   4   5

Overall—2½″ long, 3″ wide; large wing—1½″ long, 1″ wide; small wing—1¼″ long, ½″ wide.

BUTTERFLY

The butterfly is a fun thing to do. It can be made in many colors, so allow your creative abilities and bold color sense to take over. Little girls adore wearing one in their hair, and by all means perch one on a flower in an arrangement.

Materials

Wings, ½ bunch beads
Body and Antennae, 1 strand of beads
Wires, 26- or 28-gauge wire for wings; 30- or 32-gauge wire for body and antennae.

Wings

Small. BASIC: 3 beads, very pointed tops, round bottoms, 9 rows. Make 2.

Large. BASIC: 3 beads, very pointed tops, round bottoms, 11 rows. Make 2.

The wings are made with a Curved Basic. You will make 1 large wing and 1 small wing with the basic wire curving to the right. Make 1 large wing and 1 small wing with the basic wire curving to the left. Do the 2 right ones first, then the 2 left ones. *Fig. 29.* Cut open the basic loop at the base of the wing, thereby reducing the wires to 2. Combine the wings by setting 1 small right wing on top of 1 large right wing, right sides up, bottoms even, and twisting the bottom wires together. Combine the 2 left wings in the same way. Combine both pairs of wings by setting them on top of one another, right sides in, bottoms even, and twisting all wires together. Open the wings. *Fig. 30.*

Shading the Wings. The wings can be made multi-colored, tipped, or edged by feeding various colors onto the open end of your wire. (See Shading in General Instructions Chapter). For example, execute rows 1, 2, and 3 in yellow, rows 4 and 5 in black, then the remaining 4 rows in white (small wing). Execute rows 1, 2, 3, 4, and 5 in yellow, rows 6 and 7 in black, and remaining rows, 8, 9, 10, and 11, in white, (large wing). The body and antennae can be made in black.

Body

Three inches from the open end of the spool wire, make a narrow loop of 2″ of beads. Wrap around this loop with beads. *Fig. 31.* Twist the wires together.

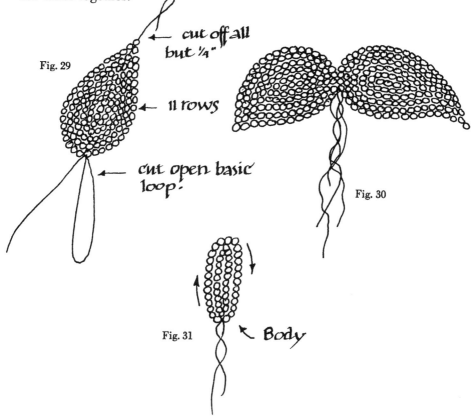

cut off all but ¼″

Fig. 29

11 rows

cut open basic loop.

Fig. 30

Fig. 31   Body

Antennae

String 2½" of beads (same color as the body) on assembly wire. Coil the open end of the assembly wire three times around the pointed end of a crewel or darning needle. Keep the coils close. Remove the needle from the coil. Push 1¼" of beads to the base of the coiled wire. Make a basic loop at the base of the 1¼" of beads so that the 1¼" of beads are tight between the coiled wire and the basic loop. Measure another 1¼" of beads and coil bare wire 3 times around the point of the needle. Remove needle, cut wire close to the top of the coil, cut off excess wire at the top of the first coil, cut open the basic loop at the base of the loop and twist the 2 wires together. Combine the body and antennae by twisting their wires together. Straighten the antennae forward, and the body to the back. *Fig. 32, 33.*

Combine the wings and the body antennae unit by setting the body and antennae in between the 2 pairs of wings. Aim the antennae to the front, and the body and small wings to the back. Shape the wings up and out and tape to a piece of taped stem wire (16-gauge) or to a hair clip or bobby pin.

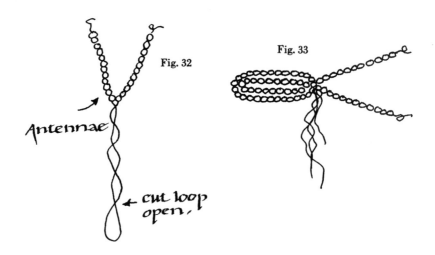

Fig. 32

Fig. 33

Antennae

← cut loop open.

Flower—6½" wide.
See also Plate XI.

CABBAGE ROSE

This glamorous interpretation of the old-fashioned ROSA CENTIFOLIA has a flower 7" wide which should be mounted on 3 long 16-gauge wires. A true showpiece, it is particularly handsome in red, pink, yellow or white. The velvet pot is made with black velvet tubing that has been glued around an ordinary clay pot.

Materials
Petals, 5 bunches beads
Leaves, 1 bunch green beads
Wires, 26- or 28-gauge wire

Petals
All petals have round tops and round bottoms.

BASIC: 5 beads, 11 rows. Make 2 for each flower.
BASIC: 5 beads, 13 rows. Make 2 for each flower.
BASIC: 7 beads, 17 rows. Make 3 for each flower.
BASIC: 10 beads, 21 rows. Make 3 for each flower.
BASIC: 10 beads, 25 rows. Make 5 for each flower.
BASIC: 10 beads, 29 rows. Make 6 for each flower.

Lace all 21-, 25-, and 29-row petals individually.

Sepals
BASIC: 14 beads, pointed tops, round bottoms, 7 rows.
    Make 7 in green.

Leaves
BASIC: 6 beads, pointed tops, round bottoms, 11 rows.
    Make 15 leaves and tape their stem wires.

Fig. 34

41

Assembly of Flowers

Cup the 2 smallest petals with the wrong side in. Entwine them so that the petals nestle inside one another. *Fig. 34.* Twist the bottom wires together and tape them.

Cut 3 16-gauge wires 14″ long. Tape them individually, then tape them together for extra strength. To the top of these 3 wires, tape the 2 small petals. Cut a 20″ piece of assembly wire and attach one end of it at the base of the petals. Wrap the wire several times, very tightly. Shape all petals, before assembling, by cupping all of them, right side in, then softly rolling the outer edge at the top, outward. Add the petals, one at a time, smallest ones first, all around the base of the flower. With each addition of a petal, wrap the assembly wire around the stem at least twice, tightly. Cut and add more assembly wire as needed. When all petals have been added, add on the 7 sepals around the base of the flower, right side out. Thin out the wires, taper them, then cover the wires with tape. Bend the head of the flower forward.

Assembly of Leaves

Cut 3 pieces of 16-gauge wires, 9″ long. Tape them. To the top of 1 wire, tape 1 leaf. Continue taping down the stem wire for 1¼″. Add a second leaf on the left of the stem wire. Tape for ½″ and tape another leaf on the right side of the stem wire. Tape down another 1¼″, add another leaf on the left. Tape down the stem for ½″ and add the fifth leaf. Make three sprigs with 5 leaves each. *Fig. 35.*

After attaching the leaf sprigs to stem of the rose, then shape the leaves by giving them a gentle twist. Wrap small green beads around the entire stem if desired. Use assembly wire for stringing. Insert flower stem into the pot to the base of the beading on the stem.

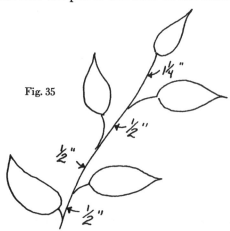

Fig. 35

Spray—12" high; small flower—¾" high, 1" wide; medium flower—
1¼" high, 1¼" wide; large flower—1½" high, 1¾" wide.

CANTERBURY BELLS

Canterbury bells (CAMPANULA MEDIUM) add grace to any floral arrangement, and are lovely grouped by themselves. Their natural color is, of course, blue, but they are just as beautiful in white, lavender, yellow or pink. The stamens can be made in either black, pale yellow, or pale green, depending on which color blends best with the rest of the arrangement.

Materials

Flowers, seven 20" strings

Stamen, 96 black beads

Leaves, and Calyx, ½ bunch green beads

Work bells, stamens, and calyx on 28-gauge wire, and leaves on 26-gauge wire. Use 16-gauge wire for mounting the spray.

Flowers

Leave 3" of wire at both ends of each flower.

Small. Make 8 continuous loops using 1½" of beads for each loop. *Fig. 36.* Make 1 for each spray.

Medium. Make 10 continuous loops using 2" of beads for each loop. Make 3 for each spray.

43

Large. Make 12 continuous loops using 2½" of beads for each loop. Make 2 for each spray.

Stamens

Make 2 continuous single loops using 8 beads for each loop, leaving 3" of wire at the start and at the finish. Onto both wires, add ¾" of green beads, then twist the bare wires together and tape. Make 1 for each flower. *Fig. 37.*

Calyx

Use 28-gauge wire. Do not twist end wires together.

Small. Make 4 continuous loops using 1" green beads for each loop. Make 1 for each small bell.

Medium. Make 4 continuous loops using 1½" of beads for each loop. Make 1 for each medium bell.

Large. Make 6 continuous loops using 2" of beads for each loop. Make 1 for each large bell.

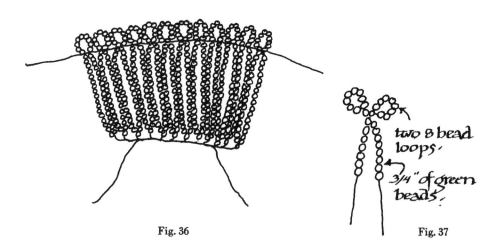

Fig. 36

two 8 bead loops.

¾" of green beads.

Fig. 37

Leaves

Use 4-row crossover loops. Use 26-gauge wire.

Small. Make a narrow loop of 2½″ of beads, bead up the front and down the back of the loop. This will give it 4 rows in all. Tape the stem wires. Make 4.

Large. Make a narrow loop of 3″ of beads, bead up the front and down the back of the loop, giving it 4 rows in all. Tape the stem wires. Make 4.

Assembly of Flowers

Each bell flower must be laced ¼″ down from the top of each loop. (See General instructions for skip lacing.) After you finish lacing each flower, shape each one outward at the bottom, bend back the beads above the lacing, close the flower, right side in so that the lacing shows on the outside. Twist the lacing wires together. Cut off all but ¼″ of the twisted wires and tuck in the remaining ¼″ of wires.

Insert a stamen into the center of each bell flower and twist the flower wires and stamen wires together. Add the correct size calyx to each bell, twist the wires together and cover the twisted wires with tape.

Assembly of Spray

Tape a 12″ piece of 16-gauge stem wire. To the top of this, tape the smallest flower, leaving 1¼″ of stem showing on the stem of the flower. Continue taping down the heavy stem wire for ¼″, then tape on 2 small leaves, one on each side of the stem wire. It is not necessary to leave any stem showing on the leaves. Tape down the stem wire for another 1¼″ and add a medium flower leaving 1¼″ of stem on each flower. Tape down the stem wire for 1¼″ and add another small leaf. Continue in this method, flower, leaf, flower, leaf, etc., until all flowers and leaves have been taped to the heavy stem wire. You will finish with 2 leaves. Cut the stem shorter if necessary.

Flower—2½" wide, 10" stem; bud—1½" long, 8" stem.
See also Plate V.

CARNATION

Carnations have a charm which have made them popular in England and America. Picotee carnations are usually edged in pink in contrast to the rest of the flower; Bizarre carnations have several stripes of contrasted colors. Carnations are often dyed by florists, so even if you are a purist about horticultural fidelity, consider this a license to make bead carnations in any desired color.

Materials

Flower and bud, eight 20" strands of beads in color, on 28-gauge wire.

Leaves and calyx, 6 strands of green

Wire, 28-gauge for all flower parts and leaves; 16-gauge for stems; 32-gauge for assembly

Flower

The carnation has 4 separate units, but several sections to each unit. Make each new loop close to the preceding one as you work, and make each section separately. *Fig. 38.* Leave 3" of wire at the start and at the finish of each section.

Unit 1. Make 5 continuous single loops, and measure 1¼" of beads for each loop. Each loop, when finished will measure ⅝". Make 3.

Unit 2. Make 5 continuous loops, and measure 1½" of beads for each loop. Each loop, when finished, will measure ¾″. **Make 5.**

Unit 3.   Make 7 continuous single loops, and measure 1¾″ of beads for each loop. Each loop, when finished will measure ⅞″. **Make 2.**

Unit 4.   Make 7 continuous single loops, and measure 2″ of beads for each loop. The loops, when finished, will measure 1″. **Make 4.**

Bud

Make 3 continuous single loops, measuring 2½″ of beads for each loop. Narrow the loops and twist them together.

Leaves

Small. BASIC: 2″, pointed tops, round bottoms, 3 rows.
    Make 7.

Large. BASIC: 3″, pointed tops, round bottoms, 3 rows.
    Make 3.

Reduce the number of wires at the base of all leaves to 2 by cutting open the basic loop at the base of the leaf, then tape the wires.

Bud Calyx

BASIC: 1¼″, pointed tops, round bottoms, 3 rows. Make 4 for each bud. Reduce the bottom wires to 2. Do not tape the stems.

Flower Calyx

Make 8 continuous single loops, measuring 2½″ of beads for each loop. The loops, when finished, will measure 1¼″. You will need 1 for each flower. This calyx needs lacing, and it can be done by skip lacing.

Cut a 15″ piece of assembly wire. Insert one end of it into the

Fig. 38

center of loop 1, one-third of the way up from the bottom of the loop. Wrap the long end of the wire completely around loop 1. Wrap under loop 1 and loop 2, over the top of loop 2, under and over loop 3, under and over loop 4, and under and over loop 5, etc., until all loops have been laced. Pull each loop close to the preceding one, and keep the loops in a straight line. Then, when all of the loops have been skip-laced, fold the calyx in half—wrong side in— and twist the lacing wires together for ¼". Cut off all but the part that is twisted, and tuck the twisted portion inside the calyx. Do not twist the bottom wires. Let them hang straight. Bell out the top two-thirds of the loops of the calyx to shape it.

Assembly of Flower

Shape the parts of each unit before putting the flower together. Start with the 3 sections of Unit 1. Have the loops pear shaped, and twist the wires together 2 or 3 times only. Treat the 5 sections of Unit 2 in the same manner.

For the 2 sections of Unit 3, and the 4 sections of Unit 4, narrow the loops, and give the tip of each loop a half twist. Gather the loops upward, so the bottoms are in a straight line, then bring the end wires to the center of the section, and twist them together. Tape a 10" piece of 16-gauge wire, and set it aside. *Fig. 39.*

Stack the 3 sections of Unit 1, one on top of the other, so that the bottoms are even, and twist all bottom wires together. Cut off all but ½" of the wires and cover these wires with tape. Tape this unit to the top of the 16-gauge stem wire. Cut a piece of assembly wire (20") and attach it to the base of Unit 1 by wrapping it very tightly at the base of the Unit 3 or 4 times. Use this wire for adding all the remaining sections of the flower, and wrap the wire very tightly,

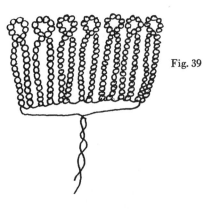

Fig. 39

twice, as each additional section is added. Start with the 5 sections of Unit 2, making them fit snugly around the base of Unit 1. Add the 2 sections of Unit 3, opposite each other, making them fit snugly around the base of the preceding units. Add the 4 sections of Unit 4 in the same manner. When all units have been added, wrap, 3 or 4 times more with the assembly wire, and cut away the excess. Cover the bare wires with one width of tape (½") and cut away all excess wires that extend below the bottom of the tape.

Assembly of Bud

Cover the bare wires of the bud with tape, and tape it directly to the top of an 8" piece of taped 16-gauge wire. To the base of the bud loops, tape the bud calyx leaves all around the bud loops. Thin out the wires to eliminate bulkiness, and finish covering the calyx wires with tape. Tape the leaf stems, and tape on 3 small leaves to the bud stem. Tape on a pair of them 1½" below the base of the bud. Tape on a single leaf 1½" below the pair, no leaf stem showing.

Insert the stem on the flower into the center of the calyx. Push the calyx up to the base of the flower as far as possible, and cover the calyx wires with tape to hold it firmly to the base of the carnation.

Adding Leaves to Carnation Stem

Attach a piece of tape to the flower stem 1½" below the bottom of the flower. At this point add, with tape, a pair of small leaves, setting them opposite each other, right side up. Tape down the stem for 1¼" and add another pair of small leaves, opposite each other, right side up. Tape down the stem for another 1½" and tape on a pair of large leaves, opposite each other and right side up. Set the leaves flush to the master stem, with no leaf stem showing. Attach, with tape, the bud stem ½" below the pair of large leaves on the carnation stem. At this point, tape on the third large leaf, and finish taping to the bottom of the flower stem.

Shaping

Bend the head of the carnation forward. Curl each leaf, right side out, around your finger.

Spray—12″ high.
See also Plate VI.

CHINESE OR JAPANESE LANTERNS

The inflated calyx of the fruit of PHYSALIS ALKEKENGI is a vivid orange in autumn. As the lanterns are easy to make, exotic and dramatic effects can be achieved with a minimum of effort. Six lanterns and 5 groups of 4 leaves each will produce a generous spray.

Materials

Lanterns, 1 bunch orange beads
Leaves, 1 bunch green beads
Wires, 28-gauge for flowers and leaves; 16-gauge for stem
Tape, use brown or twig

Petals

BASIC: 8 beads, pointed tops, round bottoms, 9 rows. Work with a long basic loop—about 8″. Make 3 petals for each lantern.

Leaves

Small. BASIC: 3 beads, pointed tops, round bottoms, 9 rows. Make 5.

Medium. BASIC: 6 beads, pointed tops, round bottoms, 11 rows. Make 10.

Large. BASIC: 9 beads, pointed tops, round bottoms, 15 rows. Make 5.

Assembly of Flowers

Stack all 3 petals for each lantern—one on top of the other—right side up. Twist together the stem wires. Turn the petals wrong side in. Bow out the bottom of the petals, and bow in the tops of the petals until the tips touch. Catch the tips of these 3 petals together with a small piece of 30- or 32-gauge wire. Twist the wires together, cut off all but ¼" and tuck this ¼" of wire inside the lantern. Tape the stem wires and arch them. *Fig. 40.*

Fig. 40

Assembly of Leaves

Tape the leaf stems individually, then tape together 1 small leaf and 1 medium leaf 1" below the base of the leaf. *Fig. 41*. To this add, with tape, 1 medium and 1 large leaf in between the first 2 leaves, leaving 1" of stem on both. *Fig. 42*. Make 5 groupings in the same manner.

Assembly of Spray

Tape a 12" piece of 16-gauge wire. At the top, attach with tape, 1 grouping of 4 leaves, leaving 1" of stem on the leaf grouping. Tape down the heavy stem wire for 1½" and add a lantern, leaving 2" of stem wire on the lantern. Tape down the heavy stem wire for another 1½" and add another grouping of 4 leaves. Continue in this manner until the spray has been completely assembled. This is a full spray and variations can be made simply by adding more leaves and lanterns for larger ones or subtracting for shorter ones.

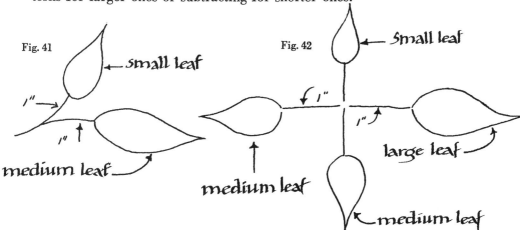

Fig. 41

small leaf

1"

medium leaf

Fig. 42

small leaf

1"

1"

large leaf

medium leaf

medium leaf

Flower—4½″ wide.
See also Plate IX.

CHRYSANTHEMUM (Football Mums)

"Mum" is florists' slang for chrysanthemum, and the correct botanical name for this immense flower is CHRYSANTHEMUM MORIFOLIUM. Blooms are available in many colors—browns, oranges, rusts, reds, yellows, and whites, as well as lavenders and pinks. Despite their large size, football mums are comparatively easy to make.

There are 7 units to each flower. The flower is exceptionally attractive if Units 1 and 2 are made in a contrast color. Leave 3″ of bare wire at the beginning and at the end of each unit.

Materials

Flower, 3 bunches beads
Leaves, 1 bunch green beads
Wires, four 16-gauge wires for stem
   26- or 28-gauge for all parts of flowers and leaves
   32-gauge for lacing

Flower

Unit 1. Make 3 continuous single loops, measuring 1¾″ of beads for each loop. Make 1.

Unit 2. Make 7 continuous single loops, measuring 2¼″ of beads for each loop. Make 1.

Unit 3. Units 3 through 7 require quite a few loops, and they are easier to handle if the number of loops are divided into 2 units. We will set the pattern for Unit 3, and you can apply this information to Units 4, 5, 6, and 7.

Unit 3 calls for 12 continuous 4-row crossover loops, measuring 3″ of beads for the initial loop, then beading up the front and down the back of the single loop. (See the General Instructions Chapter.) If you do 6 four-row crossover loops, cut the loops from the spool of wire, repeat it, and join the 2 sections together, you will have accomplished the same thing and the unit is much easier to manipulate. Join the 2 sections by placing one on top of the other, loops up and wires down, then twisting the pairs of wires together. Unfold it into a circle of 12 four-row crossover loops. *Fig. 43.*

Unit 4 calls for 14 continuous 4-row crossover loops, each initial loop, before the crossover, measuring 3¾″ of beads for each loop. Divide the unit into 2 sections of 7 crossover loops each and join them.

Unit 5 calls for 16 continuous 4-row crossover loops, each initial loop measuring 4½″ of beads for each loop. Divide it, and make 2 sections of 8 four-row crossover loops.

Unit 6 consists of 20 continuous *single* loops, each loop measuring 5¼″ of beads for each loop. Divide it, and make 2 sections of 10 loops each and join them.

Unit 7 consists of 20 continuous 4-row crossover loops, each initial loop measuring 5½″ of beads for each loop. Divide it, and make 2 sections of 10 each and join them.

Bud in color of flower

BASIC: 3 beads, round top, round bottom, 12 rows. Make 1 for each flower. *Fig. 44.*

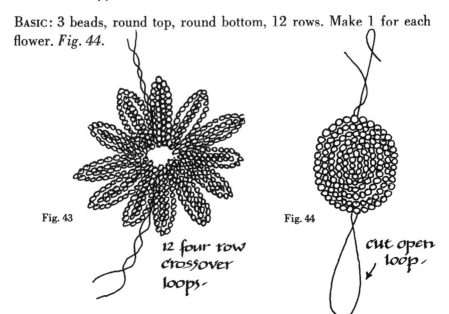

Fig. 43

12 four row crossover loops-

Fig. 44

cut open loop.

Because the bud calls for an even number of rows, you will be finishing at the top of the petal, where the single wire is. It you cut open the basic loop at the bottom of the loop, you will have two wires at both top and bottom of the petal. Bring these wires to the center of the wrong side of the petal, and twist them together.

Leaves

BASIC: 1¼", pointed top, round bottom, 5 rows. Make 7.

After executing the above, continue on same wire, making 2 loopbacks, one on the left side of the 5-row unit and one on the right side. Both loopbacks should reach to the top of the basic row. Continue, and make 2 more loopbacks—one on the left, and one on the right. This second pair of loopbacks should reach to the middle of the basic row. *Fig. 45.* Reduce the wires at the base of each leaf by cutting open the basic loop at the bottom of the leaf. Trim off the top basic wire, as usual. Tape the stems.

Bud Calyx

Make 12 continuous single loops, measuring 2" of beads for each loop. Make a circle of the loops by twisting the end wires together. Insert the stem wires of the bud into the center of the calyx, setting the bud all the way in, then twist the 2 sets of wires together to form the stem of the bud. Cover the wires with tape. Cup the loops over the bud. Make 1 in green for each bud.

Flower Calyx

BASIC: 9 beads, round top, round bottom, 12 rows. Make 1 green calyx for each flower.

After executing the second row, insert a round pencil in between the two rows of beads and make a round circle of them. *Fig. 46.* Continue wrapping beads around this circle of beads until you have 12 rows in all. Because the calyx calls for an even number of rows, you will finish at the top of the circle, where the single wire is. Cut the wire from the spool, open the basic loop at the bottom of the loop, and twist both pairs of wires together. Bring these wires through the open circle from the wrong side to the right side.

Assembly of Flower

Place Unit 1 into the center of Unit 2 and twist the wires together, very tightly. Insert the combined Units 1 and 2 into the center of Unit 3 and twist the wires together. Insert the combined Units 1, 2, and 3 into the center of Unit 4 and twist the wires. Continue until all but the 7th unit is added. The 7th unit needs to be laced before it is added. If Unit 7 is laced, the entire flower will be much firmer.

To lace Unit 7, cut a 12″ piece of assembly wire, and thread it into a large darning needle. With a running stitch, sew 2 rows at a time, ¼ up from the bottom of the loops. Sew all the way around the unit. When the sewing is finished, remove the needle, and pull the lacing wires together until the unit is slightly cupped. Then twist the lacing wires together, cut off all but ½″ and tuck the ½″ of twisted wire inside the unit. Insert the combined units of the flower into the center of Unit 7, and twist the wires together. Cup all loops inward to form a semi-ball.

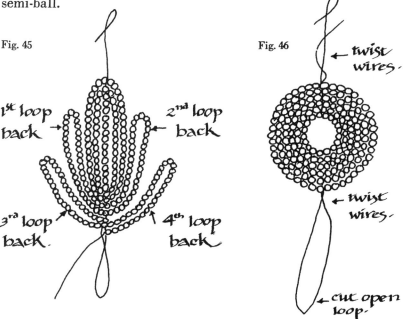

Fig. 45

1st loop back →

2nd loop ← back

3rd loop back.

4th loop back

Fig. 46

← twist wires.

← twist wires.

← cut open loop.

Stemming Flowers and Leaves

Cut 2 pieces of 16-gauge wires to the desired length for the stem of the flower. Tape them individually, then together for extra strength. Insert one end of the double stem wire into the base of the flower as far as it will go. Tape on, very securely. Insert the bottom of the stem wire into the wrong side of the flower calyx. Push the calyx up to the base of the flower as far as it will go, and tape the calyx wires to the flower stem.

Cut 2 more pieces of 16-gauge wires 9″ long for the 2 leaf branches and tape them. To the top of each wire, tape a leaf. Show ½″ of leaf stem. Tape down the stem for 1½″ and tape on another leaf, setting it on the left side of the stem wire. Tape down another 1½″ and tape on a third leaf, leaving ½″ of stem wire on all leaves. Make another spray of leaves in the same manner.

Six inches below the base of the flower—on the left side of the flower stem—tape on one spray of leaves. Tape down for another 1″ and tape on the bud. Allow 2½″ to 3″ of stem on the bud. Tape down 1½″ and add the second spray of leaves.

The stem of the flower may be wrapped with small green beads strung on assembly wire if you desire (see Tulip and Iris stemming).

Flower—3″ wide.
See also Plate VII, X.

DAFFODIL

Daffodils are NARCISSI, horticulturally speaking. Make them in all-yellow tones (pale or deep) or in blends of yellow and white, and use them as a center of interest in a spring bouquet.

Materials

Flowers, ½ bunch beads
Leaves, 1½ strands for each leaf
Wires, 28-, 32-, and 16-gauge

Petals

BASIC: 12 beads, pointed tops, round bottoms, 9 rows. Make 6 for each flower.

Crown

Make 12 continuous single loops, measuring 3″ of beads for each loop. Keep the loops close together, and narrow. Skip lace the top ¼″ of each loop. Close the unit by folding it in half, wrong side out. Twist assembly wire (lacing wires) together, cut off all but ¼″ and tuck in the ¼″ of twisted wire. Twist the bottom wires together. Make 1 for each flower. *Fig. 47.*

To shape the crown, bow out the bottom of the crown. Use the eraser end of a pencil. Bow out the sides, and bend the top ends of the loops above the lacing outward to form a fluted effect at the top of the crown.

Stamen

Two inches from the open end of the spool wire make 2 continuous loops, using 10 black beads for each loop. Onto both end wires feed 1¼″ of green beads, then twist together the two end wires so that the green beads are up close to the black loops. Tape the wires. Make 1 for each flower. *Fig. 48.*

Assembly of Flower

Cut a 10″ piece of 16-gauge wire and tape it. Tape the stem wire to the base of the green beads of the stamen. Insert the other end of the stem wire into the top of the crown. Secure the crown by taping its wires to the stem wire. Wrap a 15″ piece of assembly wire around the base of the crown and add the flower petals, one at a time, right sides up, wrapping twice tightly with the addition of each petal. Set the base of each petal close to the base of the crown. Cut away all excess petal wires 1½″ below the base of the flower. Cover the remaining wires with tape. Bend the head of the flower forward and arch the petals up and out.

Leaves

BASIC: 4″, pointed tops, round bottoms, 7 rows. Make 2 for each flower.

Cut open the basic loop at the bottom of the loop. Tape the wires.

Tape on 2 leaves, opposite one another about 5″ below the base of the flower.

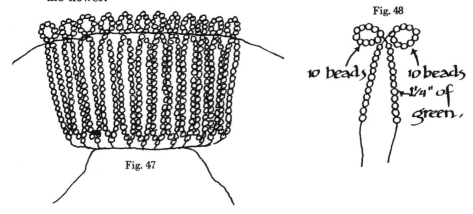

Fig. 48

10 beads   10 beads
1¼″ of green.

Fig. 47

Flower—4½" wide.
See also Plate VI.

DAHLIA

Dahlias (pronounced dahl' ya or day' li-ya) come in many sizes and colors: orange, white, yellow, red, pink, salmon, purple, russet, and the miniatures are often bicolored.

Materials

Flower, 3 bunches beads in color
Leaves, 1 bunch green
Wire, four 16-gauge stem wires for mounting flowers and leaves; 26- or 28-gauge wire for flowers and leaves

Flower

The dahlia is made exactly the same way as the chrysanthemum. The count for all of the units is the same with one exception. All units for the flower are made with continuous single loops instead of 4-row crossovers. However, Unit 7 is made with 4-row crossover loops. The leaves, bud calyx, and flower calyx are the same, and so is the assembly. The single loops of the dahlia have a softer, lacier look. Keep the loops narrow, and give each loop a half twist about ½" from the outer end of each loop. Lace Unit 7 the same as for the Chrysanthemum.

Flower—2″ wide; leaf—3″ long.
See also Plate I, IV.

DAISY

The name daisy is applied to many different flowers. This one is the traditional BELLIS PERENNIS. It is most adaptable to any arrangement of informal spring flowers. In nature, the colors are white or pink with a yellow center. A black-eyed susan is orange with a black center.

Materials

Flower, 2 strands beads for each flower
Centers, ½ strand for each
Leaves, 1 strand for each
Wires, 26- or 28-gauge for flower, leaves, and centers; 19-gauge for beaded stems; 18-gauge for plain stems

Flower

This is a continuous 4-row crossover petal. Measure 2″ of beads for the initial loop, narrow the loop, then bead up the front and down the back of the loop. Continue on, without cutting the wire from the spool, and measure another 2″ of beads for the second loop. Bead up the front and down the back of this second loop. Make 9 four-row crossover petals for each flower. (See Crossover technique in General Instructions Chapter.) Balance the wires of the daisy by crossing the end wire (at the bottom of petal 9) under petal 1. Bring the wire up between petals 1 and 2, down between petals 2 and 3, under the base of petal 3, up between petals 3 and 4, and down between petals 4 and 5. Combine the beginning wire and the ending wire in the center of the underneath side of the daisy, and twist them together.

Centers

Basic: 3 beads, round tops, round bottoms, 8 rows. Make 1 for each daisy in a contrasting color. Because the center calls for an even number of rows, you will finish at the top of the unit, where the single wire is. Twist together the finish wire and the top basic wire. Cut open the basic loop at the bottom of the loop, and twist the basic loop wires together. Set the center on top of the daisy, and bring both sets of center wires to the under side of the daisy. Join them to the daisy stem wires, by twisting.

Leaves

Measure 6" of beads and form them into a narrow loop. Bead up the front and down the back of the loop for a 4-row crossover. Cut the wire from the spool, twist the wires together and tape them. Make 2 for each daisy.

Assembly

If you are using the large green stem beads, hook a piece of 19-gauge wire into the wires at the base of the flower, tape the wires for ½", cut away excess flower wires, cover the taped part of the wires with small green beads strung on assembly wire, then bead the rest of the stem with the large green stem beads for 3, 4, or 5". Cover the remaining stem wire with tape. Tape on 2 leaves at the base of the large stem beads. If you are not beading the stems, merely tape a piece of stem wire to the base of the flower, and add 2 leaves to the stem wire 4" below the base of the flower.

1   2   3   4   5

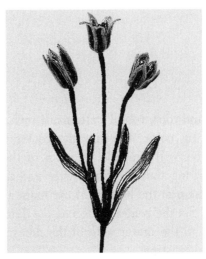

Flower—2½" high, 1½" wide; leaves—7"
long, 1⅛" wide; cluster of three—8½"
high, 6½" wide. See also Plate II.

DARWIN TULIPS

TULIPA are divided into ten major groups. There are cottage tulips, Darwin tulips, and parrot tulips to name a few, and they come in many different sizes, shapes and colors, from subtle quiet tones to gorgeous brilliantly contrasted ones. Beaded tulips can be tipped, edged, or shaded.

Materials

Flower, 1 strand beads for each petal
Leaves, 2½ to 3 strands green beads for each leaf
Wires, 16-gauge for stems; 26- or 28-gauge for flowers; 18- and 26-
* gauge for leaves*

Petals

BASIC: 1¼" pointed tops, round bottoms, 9 rows. Make 5 for each flower.

Reduce the wires at the base of all petals to 2, by cutting open the bottom basic wire at the base of the petals.

Should you wish to tip your tulip in a contrast color, work the basic row, 2, 3, 4, 5, 6, and 7½ in color #1. Allow enough bare spool wire to complete the petal and cut the wire from the spool. Feed on enough beads in the contrast color to complete the top of row 8 and the top half of row 9, then add enough beads of color #1 to finish the bottom

62

half of row 9. Should you wish to merely edge your tulip in a contrast color, work through the 7th row with color #1, allow enough bare spool wire to finish the petal, cut the wire from the spool, and feed on the open end of the wire enough beads in a contrast color to work rows 8 and 9. Should you wish to create a Parrot tulip in three colors, start with the darkest color. Make rows 1 through 3 (this includes the basic) in the dark color, measure about 20" of wire and cut the wire from the spool. Onto the open end of the wire, feed enough beads in a medium shade to work rows 4, 5, 6, and 7. Feed on enough beads in the palest color to finish working rows 8 and 9.

Suggested color combinations

Ruby red for rows 1, 2, and 3; medium orange for rows 4, 5, 6, and 7; yellow for rows 8 and 9.

Fuchsia for rows 1, 2, and 3; medium pink for rows 4, 5, 6, and 7; pale pink or white for rows 8 and 9.

Royal blue for rows 1, 2, and 3; medium blue for rows 4, 5, 6, and 7; pale blue or white for rows 8 and 9.

Lavenders and oranges may be used in the same way.

Stamen

Tulip stamens are usually black. All beaded tulips look well with black or dark brown stamens.

Make 2 continuous single loops, using 10 beads for each loop. Onto both stem wires, string 1¼" of green beads. Twist the wires together at the base of the green beads. Tape the wires. Make 1 for each flower.

Leaves

BASIC: 6", pointed tops, round bottoms, 9 rows.

These leaves are long and slim, and a bit awkward to make until you have done one or two. However, life-sized tulips need life-size leaves, so try one. If you find you are having trouble keeping the leaf flat as you work, try using one or two hair clips to keep the rows of beads close and flat. *Fig. 49.* Leave 1″ of top basic wire on all leaves. Cover this 1″ of wire with tape. Cut open the bottom basic loop at the bottom of the loop. Lace the leaf—right side up—one third of the way down from the top. Start the lacing in the middle of the basic row and lace each row, working from the center to the outside rows. Always lock the ends of the lacing wires by wrapping twice, over the wires that join the last two rows of the leaf, then cut off the lacing wires very close to the outer row beads. Tape a 10″ piece of 18-gauge wire, and tape it to taped basic wire at the top of the leaf. Bring the 18-gauge wire down the back of the leaf, and tape it to the wires at the bottom. Lace once more through the center of the leaf, and include the 18-gauge wire as you lace. Lock in the lacing wires the same way as before, and cut them off close to the beads.

Assembly of Flower

Lace all 5 petals together. Your flower will be firmer if you lace every row of beads. To lace a closed tulip, lace with the right side of the petals facing you. To lace an open tulip, lace with the wrong side of the petals facing you. Always start your lacing in the middle of the basic row of petal #1. When all five petals have been laced together, turn the petals around, right side still facing you; finish lacing the first few rows on petal #1. Close the tulip petals by folding them in half, wrong side of the lacing in, and twist together the 2 ends of the lacing wire. Twist them for ¼″ and cut away the excess wire. Tuck the remaining twisted ¼″ of wire inside the tulip. Twist the bottom petal wires together, and shape the tulip by bowing out the petals at the bottom of the flower so that the rows of beads are even, and the petals do not overlap. If you have made an open tulip, close it in the same way, then shape by bowing out the bottoms of the petals at the base of the flower, and bending the tips outward.

Tape a 10 or 12″ piece of 16-gauge wire, and tape the stamen to the top of it. Insert the opposite end of the stem wire into the top of the tulip until the green beads of the stamen reach the bottom of the flower. Tape stem and flower wires together, firmly for 1½″. Cut off the excess petal wires. Wrap the flower stem with green beads that have been strung on 30- or 32-gauge wire. (See Beaded Stems.)

Wrap the flower stem for approximately 8″. Wrap the fine wire around the stem 2 or 3 times and cut the wire from the spool. It takes nearly 3 strands of beads to wrap the stem of 1 tulip, so pre-string at least that much before starting.

Assembly of Arrangement

Tulips are much easier to pot and arrange if they are combined in groups of 2 or 3. If you are grouping 3 flowers, you will need 4 leaves. If you are grouping 2 flowers, you will need 3 leaves. Each individual tulip should have 2 leaves. When you group the tulips, bind them together with tape at the base of the beaded stems. Add the leaves, one at a time, at the base of the beaded stems. Add leaves for single tulips directly below the beaded stems also, setting one on the left side of the stem, and the other on the right side, directly opposite the first one. When potting tulips, set them deeply enough into the container so that there is no stem showing below the leaves.

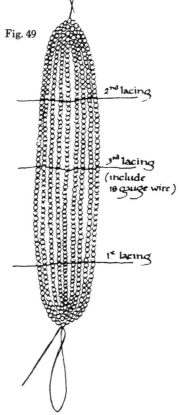

Fig. 49

2ⁿᵈ lacing

3ʳᵈ lacing
(include
18 gauge wire)

1ˢᵗ lacing

Flower—2½" wide.
See also Plate IX.

DAY LILY

The day lily (HEMEROCALLIS) is smaller than the tiger lily to which it is similar. It can be used singly or in groups of twos and threes in floral arrangements, or it can be potted as a smaller version of the tiger lily. Its natural colors are yellow and orange and rust, with either black, brown or deep orange stamens.

Materials

Petals, approximately 3 strands per flower
Stamens, approximately 6" of a contrast color per flower
Wires, 26- or 28-gauge for all parts
 16-gauge for stems

Petals

BASIC: 1¼", pointed tops, round bottoms, 7 rows. Make 6 for each flower.
Reduce the basic wires to 2 on each petal, by cutting open the bottom basic loop at the base of each petal.

Stamen

Make a narrow loop with 15 beads, and give this loop a 4-row crossover by beading up the front and down the back of the loop. Twist the bottom wires together, twice, tightly, very close to the bottom of the loop. Cut off one wire very close to the base of the loop. Onto the remaining wire, put 1½" of green beads. Make 3 for each flower. When the three stamens have been completed, combine the three wires and twist them together, tightly, so that the green beads are close to the base of the crossover loops. *Fig. 50.*

Assembly of Flower

Stack 6 petals, right side up, so that they are even at the bottom. Twist the wires together. Make a circle of the petals. Shape them by bending the petals up at the bottom and out at the top. Slide the 3 stamens in between 2 petals, and twist the stamen wires around the petal wires. Tape the wires.

Leaves

Make a narrow loop of 4″ of beads. Give this loop a 4-row crossover by beading up the front of the loop, and down the back. Twist the bottom wires together and tape them. Make at least 2 for each flower.

Stemming

Use taped 16-gauge wire cut to the desired length, an 8″ or 9″ piece should be sufficient. Tape the base of the flower directly to the top of the stem wire. Add leaves 2″ and 4″ down the stem, in pairs, no stem showing on the leaves.

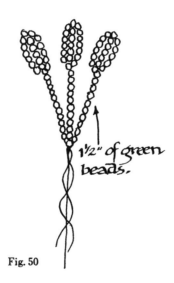

1½″ of green beads.

Fig. 50

Spray—15″ high, 4½″ wide at
base. See also Plate V.

DELPHINIUM

The delphinium or larkspur is valuable in any two-sided or four-sided floral arrangement, because its blossoms encircle the master stem which eliminates the necessity of duplicating the center flowers. It is distinctive because of its broad conical spike, and large individual flowers. This pattern is life size, but the number of flowers can be increased or decreased, depending on the height or width of your arrangement. The petals of the flowers can be executed in 1 solid color, or they may be divided into 2 or 3 colors. For example: the blossoms in Units 1 and 2 require 4 petals each. If you have planned a blue delphinium, make 1 petal in dark blue, 2 petals in medium blue, and 1 petal in white. For the 3-petal blossoms, make 1 petal in each color, and for the 2-petal blossoms, make 1 in each of blues, as these represent the buds at the top of the spike, and they are usually darker in color. You need not confine your delphinium to blue, although this is its most popular natural color. Pinks with white, yellows with white or pale orange, and blends of lavenders and purples make up most attractively. The centers, usually yellow, will be apparent even in a flower made with white and yellow tones.

Materials

Flowers and stamens, about 2½ bunches beads
Leaves, about 1 bunch green
Wires, 28-gauge for flowers and stamens; 26- or 28-gauge for leaves;
  double 16-gauge for stem

Flower

BASIC: 4 beads, round tops and round bottoms, for all size petals.

Unit 1. 11 rows; 5 flowers with 4 petals each.
Unit 2. 9 rows; 5 flowers with 4 petals each.
Unit 3. 7 rows; 4 flowers with 4 petals each.
Unit 4. 7 rows; 4 flowers with 3 petals each.
Unit 5. 7 rows; 3 flowers with 2 petals each.
Reduce to 2 the number of wires at the base of each petal by cutting
open the basic loop at the base of the petal.

Because of the many sizes involved, it is suggested that as each
unit is finished, you label it in an envelope of its own. When you are
ready to assemble the flower, it will be much easier to tell one unit
from the other.

Stamens

Make 1 for each flower using a contrasting color.

Units 1 and 2. Make 4 continuous single loops measuring 1¼" of
beads for each loop.

Unit 3. Make 4 continuous single loops, measuring 1" of beads for
each loop.

Unit 4. Make 3 continuous loops measuring 1" of beads for each
loop.

Unit 5. Make 1 loop with 1" of beads.

Leaves

Small. BASIC: 10 beads, pointed tops, round bottoms, 7 rows. Make
10.

Medium. BASIC: 10 beads, pointed tops, round bottoms, 9 rows. Make 10.

Large. BASIC: 12 beads, pointed tops, round bottoms, 13 rows. Make 10.

Reduce the number of wires at the base of each leaf to 2, by cutting open the basic loop at the base of the leaf. Tape the leaf stems. Keep the leaves in separate groups, according to size, and label them. Assembly will be easier.

Assembly of Flowers

For the 4-petal flowers—stack 4 petals, one on top of the other, right side up, bottoms even, and twist the wires together. Fan out the petals to form a circle, then cup the petals inward. Insert the proper size stamen into the center of the flower, and wrap the stamen wires around the petal wires. Cover the wires with tape.

Assemble the 3-petal flowers and corresponding stamens in the same way. Assemble the 2-petal flowers by having the 2 small petals face one another, *wrong* side in. Cup them inward, slightly. Slide the stamen into the center, twist the wires together, and cover them with tape.

Assembly of Spike

Cut two 16-gauge wires to the desired length (about 12 to 14"). Tape them individually, then tape them together for extra strength. Attach a generous piece of tape to the top of the heavy stem wire and tape on a small leaf. Tape ½" down the stem and add another small leaf. Tape down the stem for another ½" and add flower of Unit 5. Continue taping on flowers and leaves, starting with the small ones, and gradually add the larger ones. It is important that you add flowers and leaves *around* the master stem as well as down. So that the spike will grow not only in length but also in width, leave stems on the flowers—about ½" on the small flowers to 2½" on the larger ones. Finish the assembly with 2 or 3 leaves at the base of all the other blossoms and leaves. Make them the large size leaves. Tape down to the bottom of the master stem.

Branch—18″ high.

EUCALYPTUS

These enormous leaves are often colored and sent East from California, where they grow, as winter decorations.

Materials

1 bunch green beads

Wires, 26- or 28-gauge for leaves; one 14″ piece of 16-gauge wire for stem

Leaves

These leaves all have round tops and round bottoms.

Unit 1. BASIC: 5 beads, 5 rows. Make 1.

Unit 2. BASIC: 5 beads, 7 rows. Make 2.

Unit 3. BASIC: 5 beads, 11 rows. Make 2.

Unit 4. BASIC: 5 beads, 15 rows. Make 2.

Unit 5. BASIC: 7 beads. 19 rows. Make 6.

Unit 6. same as Unit 4. BASIC: 5 beads, 15 rows. Make 2 more.

Unit 7. same as Unit 5. BASIC: 7 beads, 19 rows. Make 6 more.

Cut open the basic loop at the base of the leaf, reducing your bottom wires to 2. Keep the units separated. If you do, your assembly will be much easier.

Assembly

Tape a 14″ piece of 16-gauge wire. To the top of it, tape the smallest leaf (Unit 1). Tape down the stem for ½″ and add the 2 leaves of Unit 2, directly opposite each other—no leaf stem showing. Tape down the stem for ¾″ and add the 2 leaves of Unit 3, directly opposite one another, no leaf stem showing. Continue adding the leaves in pairs, until you have taped on all the leaves of all the units. Arrange the leaves so that they are horizontal to the stem wire.

Flower—3" wide. See also Plate IV.

FANTASIA

The Fantasia, a composite of 2 flowers that are native to the Caribbean Islands, is the result of some drawings I made during a trip to the West Indies. It is so named because of the reaction so many of my pupils had when they first saw it. "Fantastic," they said, and so it became the Fantasia. It resembles several flowers but isn't a true copy of any. An ambitious flower that entails quite a bit of work, the technique is simple, and the results are gratifying. The petals are particularly attractive when edged in a contrast color, as it gives them depth. The flower can be used either for height on long stems or for fullness when they are mounted on shorter stems.

Materials

Petals, 1½ bunches beads in color
Leaves, 1 bunch green beads
Wire, 26- or 28-gauge for all parts; 16-gauge wire for stems

Petals

Unit 1. BASIC: 1¼", round tops, round bottoms, 7 rows. Make 4 in a solid color (no edging).

Unit 2. Basic: 1¼", pointed tops, round bottoms, 5 rows. Make 15 with edging.

Make the basic row and rows 2 and 3 in a pale color. Allow 10" of bare spool wire at the completion of the third row, and cut the wire from the spool. Onto this 10" extension of wire, feed enough beads in a contrast color to complete rows 4 and 5. Reduce the number of wires at the base of each petal to 2 by cutting open the basic loop at the base of each petal. Do not tape individual petal stems.

Unit 3. Basic: 2¼", pointed tops, round bottoms, 5 rows. Make 18. Make these petals in the same way as for the petals in Unit 2, changing the color for rows 4 and 5, and reducing to 2 the number of wires at the base of each petal.

Centers

The centers are made in the color bead that was used for the edging of the petals.

Make 10 continuous single loops, measuring 1½" of beads for each loop. Keep the loops narrow. Make another section using the same measurements. Set one section inside the other and twist all wires together. Crush the loops upward. Cut off all but 2" of the stem wires and cover them with tape.

Bud

Unit 1. Using the light colored bead, make 10 continuous single loops, measuring 1¼" of beads for each loop. Have 4" of wire at the beginning and end of the unit. Make 1 for each bud.

Unit 2. In the deep color that was used for the edging of the petals, make 10 continuous single loops, measuring 1½" of beads for each loop. Have 4" of wire at the beginning and end of the unit. Set Unit 1 inside of Unit 2, and twist the four wires together. Cover the wires with tape. Make 1 for each bud.

Calyx

Make 11 continuous single loops, measuring 3" of beads for each loop. Work the loops close together at the bottom and make two sets.

When both sets of loops have been completed, twist one set of wires together so as to form one long unit of 22 loops. *Fig. 51.* Skip

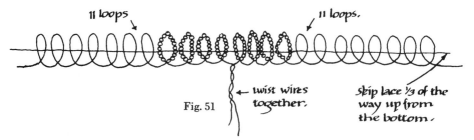

Fig. 51

lace the 22 loops with assembly wire one third of the way up from the bottoms of the loops. It's the same method of lacing as for the calyx of the carnation, the bells on the Bells of Ireland and Canterbury Bells. Fold the loops in half, wrong side in, and twist the lacing wires together for ½". Cut away all but ¼" of this wire, and tuck the ¼" of twisted wire to the inside of the calyx. Curve the loops up and out, slightly. Do not twist bottom wires together.

Flower Leaves

BASIC: 13 beads, round tops and bottoms, 13 rows. Make 5. Tape the stems.

Bud Leaves

BASIC: 10 beads, round tops and bottoms, 5 rows. Make 5. Tape the stems.

Assembly of Flower

Cut 2 pieces of 16-gauge wire to the desired length for the flower stem. Tape both wires individually, then tape them together, side by side, for extra strength. Attach a piece of tape to the top of the stem wire. Directly to the top, tape on the combined 2 units of the center. Cut a generous piece of assembly wire (about 20") and attach it to the base of the center units, wrapping 3 or 4 times, very securely.

With the assembly wire, add the 4 petals of Unit 2, one at a time, around and close to the base of the combined center units. Add the petals wrong side in, and wrap tightly with the assembly wire with each addition of a petal. Curve these 4 petals over the center loops. Add the 15 small flower petals around the base of the previously added units, right side up, wrapping tightly with each addition. Add them, one at a time. Place the base of each new petal as close as possible to the master stem, and up close to the base of the other petals. Add more asembly wire as needed. Wrap a piece of tape around the wires now and then to keep the petals and assembly wire from slipping. When all of the 15 petals have been added, wrap on the 18 large ones in the same way. Give the assembly wire a few extra wraps down the master stem, and cut off the excess. Thin out and trim off most of the petal wires, starting about 2" below the base of the flower. Cover the remaining wires with tape. Insert the flower stem into the laced calyx. Push the calyx up snugly to the base of the flower and secure by taping the calyx wires to the master stem.

Assembly of Leaves and Bud

Cut 2 pieces of 16-gauge wire about 9 or 10" long and tape them. To assemble the flower leaves, tape one large leaf to the top of one of the pieces of 16-gauge wire, leaving ½" of stem showing on the leaf. Tape down the master stem for 1½" and tape on the second leaf. Continue taping down the stem until all 5 large leaves have been added. Space them all 1½" apart on alternate sides of the wire—one to the left, one to the right, etc.

Repeat the same procedure for the bud leaves on the other piece of stem wire. When all 5 small leaves are stemmed, add the bud, leaving 2" of stem on the bud. Tape these wires to the flower stem placing the large leaves on the left, 6" below the base of the flower. To the right side, 2" lower, add the bud leaf stem. Bend the head of the flower forward, and shape each petal up and out from the center of the flower.

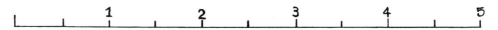

Branch—15" high.
See also Plate III, IX.

FORSYTHIA

Forsythia blossoms are among the first harbingers of spring, and their bright yellow flowers are always welcome. Short sprigs add a gay note to a mixed floral arrangement, or taller ones can be potted alone.

Materials

Flowers, yellow opaque beads
Calyx, pale green beads
Wires, 28- or 30-gauge wire for flowers and calyx; 16-gauge for stems

Flower

The following count for the flowers constitute enough blossoms for 1 sprig. Combine several sprigs to make 1 large branch.

Unit 1. 1 single 10-bead loop. Make 1.

Unit 2. 2 continuous single loops, measuring ¾" of beads for each loop. Make 3.

Unit 3. 3 continuous single loops, measuring 1" of beads for each loop. Make 3.

Unit 4. 4 continuous single loops, measuring 1¼" of beads for each loop. Make 2.

Unit 5. 4 continuous single loops, measuring 1½" of beads for each loop. Make 12.
Keep the loops of the flowers narrow.

Calyx

Unit 1. 1 single 8-bead loop. Make 1.

Unit 2. 2 continuous single 8-bead loops. Make 3.

Unit 3. 3 continuous single 8-bead loops. Make 3.

Unit 4. 4 continuous single 10-bead loops. Make 2.

Unit 5. 4 continuous single 12-bead loops. Make 12.

Assembly

Combine the flowers with their corresponding calyx by setting 1 calyx at the base of each flower. Combine the wires and twist them together. Tape the wires, using either twig or brown tape that has been cut in half, lengthwise, and stretched. For master stems, use lengths of 16-gauge wires that have also been taped. Tape on the flowers, one at a time, starting with the smallest ones. Leave ¼" of stem showing on each flower. Space the flowers about ¾" to 1" apart as you tape them to the stem wires. Vary the combinations of the sprigs.

Flower—2½″ long, 2½″ wide; spray—12″
high. See also Plate V.

FUCHSIA

The ordinary variety of fuchsia usually grows in tones of pink and
lavender or purple and fuchsia. However, there are hybrids in pure
white, soft yellow and all pink. If they are made in the bright pink
and lavender combination, the round petals should be in pink, and
the pointed petals in lavender or purple. The stamens are almost
always in black. These delicate and graceful flowers add softness and
line to any floral arrangement. The suggested count for the spray is
3 flowers and 9 leaves. The leaves are executed in three different
sizes. Should a longer spray be necessary to balance an arrangement, add an extra flower or two and add 2 of the larger leaves for
each extra flower. Follow the pattern of 2 leaves and a flower, 2 leaves
and a flower, etc., finishing off with 2 leaves.

Materials

Round petals, ½ bunch
Pointed petals, ½ bunch
Leaves, ½ bunch
Wire, 26- or 28-gauge for petals and leaves, 16-gauge for stems

Petals

Unit 1. BASIC: 3 beads, round tops, round bottoms, 13 rows. Make 3
for each flower. Work with a long basic loop (at least 8″) on all petals.

Unit 2. BASIC: 6 beads, pointed tops, round botoms, 9 rows. Make 4
for each flower.

78

Stamen

Cut three pieces of wire 6" long, and 3 pieces of wire 5" long. 26-gauge brass wire may be used in place of the silver 28- or 26-gauge if desired. In the center of each piece of wire, place 2 black beads. Twist the wires together to hold the beads in place. Twist the wires all the way to the end. Combine the stamens by stacking them so that they are even at the bottom. Twist the bottom 1½" of the wires together, and set them aside to be added to the flowers after they are assembled. This makes 6 for each flower.

Leaves

All leaves have pointed tops and round bottoms.
Small. BASIC: 7 beads, 5 rows. Make 2.
Medium. BASIC: 7 beads, 9 rows. Make 2.
Large. BASIC: 7 beads, 11 rows. Make 4.

Assembly of Flower

Cup the three round petals, wrong side in, and twist the bottom wires together, tightly, at the base of the petals. Insert the stamens into the center of the combined three up petals so that they protrude beyond the top of the petals. Cover the wires with tape for 1". Wrap one end of a 15" piece of assembly wire around the base of the petals. Wrap three times, tightly. With the assembly wire add each pointed petal, right side up, around the base of the three up petals. Wrap twice, tightly, with each addition. After the fourth petal has been added, wrap the assembly wire a few times more, then cut away any excess wire that may be longer than the stem wires of the petals.

Assembly of Flowers and Leaves on Master Stem

Tape all flower and leaf stems. Tape a 12 or 14" piece of 16-gauge stem wire. To the top of it, tape a small leaf, allowing ½" of stem on the leaf. 1" below the first leaf, tape on a second leaf, with ½" of stem showing. Tape the first flower 1" below the second leaf, leaving 1½" of stem on each flower. Continue taping the flowers and leaves down the master stem until the spray is completed, alternating the flowers and leaves as you tape. Give the spray an "S" curve when it is finished.

Stalk—17" high. See also Plate IX.

GLADIOLUS

Gladioli, or gladioluses, with their swordlike leaves and erect spikes of handsome flowers, are versatile. They can be used alone but are better used in mixed arrangements. The pattern given here is for a full spray but it can be broken up and reduced to single blossoms or shortened sprays just as though they were fresh cut flowers.

Materials

Flowers, 3 bunches color
Leaves, 2 bunches green beads
Wires, two 14-gauge wires for stem; 28- or 26-gauge for flowers, leaves, and stamens

Flowers—Extra Large

Unit 1. BASIC: 4 beads, round tops, pointed bottoms, 21 rows. Individually lace petals through the middle. Make 4.

Unit 2. BASIC: 4 beads, round tops, pointed bottoms, 19 rows. Make 1.

Flowers—Large

Unit 1. BASIC: 4 beads, round top, pointed bottoms, 19 rows. Make 4. Individually lace petals through the middle. Make 4.

Unit 2. BASIC: 4 beads, round tops, pointed bottoms, 17 rows. Make 1.

Flowers Medium

Unit 1. BASIC: 4 beads, round tops, pointed bottoms, 17 rows. Make 4.

Unit 2. BASIC: 4 beads, round tops, pointed bottoms, 15 rows. Make 1.

Flowers Small

Unit 1. BASIC: 4 beads, round tops, pointed bottoms, 15 rows. Make 4.

Unit 2. BASIC: 4 beads, round tops, pointed bottoms, 13 rows. Make 1.

Buds

Double bud and single bud. BASIC: 4 beads, round tops, pointed bottoms, 13 rows. Make 3.

Stamens

Work in a contrast color (see General Instructions Chapter). There are no stamens in the buds.

Extra large. 3 continuous single loops, 20 beads for each loop. Bead both stem wires with green beads for 1¼". Make 1.

Large. 3 continuous single loops, 18 beads for each loop. Bead both stem wires with green beads for 1". Make 1.

Medium. 3 continuous single loops, 15 beads for each loop. Bead both stem wires with green beads for 1". Make 1.

Small. 3 continuous single loops, 12 beads for each loop. Bead both stem wires with green beads for 1". Make 1.

Leaves

Small. BASIC: 1¼", pointed tops, round bottoms, 7 rows. Make 22 for 1 stalk.

These leaves will be used for calyx as well as for leaves on the stem. Lace 3 of them together for the double bud and lace 2 of them together for the single bud.

Large. BASIC: 7", pointed tops, round bottoms, 11 rows. Make 2.

Lace these long leaves individually in 2 places—⅓ of the way up from the bottom, and ⅓ of the way down from the top. Trim off all but 1″ of the top basic wire and cover this 1″ of wire with tape. Tape a 10 or 11″ piece of 18-gauge wire. Tape the 18-gauge wire to the 1″ of taped basic wire at the top of the leaf. Bring the piece of 18-gauge wire down the wrong side of the leaf and tape it to the bottom basic wires of the leaf. Lace once more through the middle of the leaf, and include the 18-gauge bracing wire, under the basic row of beads, as you lace. This bracing wire will keep the leaf firm and enable you to shape the leaf into any position.

Assembly of Flowers

Each flower is assembled in the same manner. Let's do the extra large flower. Stack 3 of the large petals (21 row) one on top of the other, right sides up, and *even* on the bottom. Twist the petal stem wires together tightly. Attach a 20″ piece of assembly wire (30- or 32-gauge) to the base of these 3 petals, wrapping it around for 3 or 4 times tightly. Shape these petals by making them concave in the center, and flared out at the top. *Fig. 52.* Swing the middle petal to the right, and the bottom petal to the left. With the assembly wire, add the fourth large petal in back of, and in between, the second and third petals. Wrap the assembly wire around 2 or 3 times very tightly. Set the stamen on the right side of the small petal so that the stem wires are even. *Fig. 53.* Twist their wires together. Add the combined small petal and stamen on top of the combined 4 petals, right sides facing each other. Wrap twice tightly with the assembly wire. Add 3 small leaves, one at a time, with the assembly wire. Place 1 leaf at the base of the small petal, add 1 leaf to the left and 1 to the right. Face them right side in. It is not necessary to add leaves to the backs of the flowers, as the flowers are set flat against the master stem. Shape the completed flower by curving the middle leaf and the small petal forward and down. Curve the other leaves forward and down. Tape the bottom wires. Combine the other 3 flowers in the same way.

Assembly of Buds

Single bud. Coil one 13 row petal, wrong side in. Insert the coiled petal into two leaves that have been laced together, closed by folding wrong side in, then twisting together the lacing wires. Cut off all but

¼" of the twisted lacing wire. Tuck to the inside the remaining ¼" of twisted wire. Push the coiled petal into the lacéd leaves as far as it will go, then cover the stem wires with tape.

Double bud. Coil two 13 row petals, wrong side in, then entwine them, one edge inside the other. Twist the stems together. Insert the double petal bud in the center of the three leaves that have been laced together, closed by folding in half and finish off as for single bud. Tape the stem wires.

Assembly of Flower Spray

Tape three 15" pieces of 16-gauge wire. Tape them individually, then tape them together for triple strength.

To the top of the master stem wire, tape 1 small leaf—no leaf stem showing. Tape down the master stem for 1" and add 1 more small leaf—no stem showing. Swing this second leaf to the left, slightly. Tape down the master stem for another inch and add a third small leaf. Swing this third leaf to the right, slightly. Add the 2 remaining small leaves in the same manner, 1 to the left, and 1 to the right. Tape down the stem for 1" and add the small bud. An inch further down the stem, tape on the large bud. Now tape on the flowers, one at a time, 1½" apart, starting with the smallest (Unit 4), then the 3rd, the 2nd, and the 1st. Should you desire a very long spray, set the flowers 2 to 2½" apart. One inch below the largest flower, tape on the 2 large spike leaves, 1 on the right side, and 1 on the left. Give the entire spray of flowers an "S" curve.

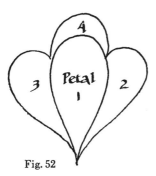

Fig. 52

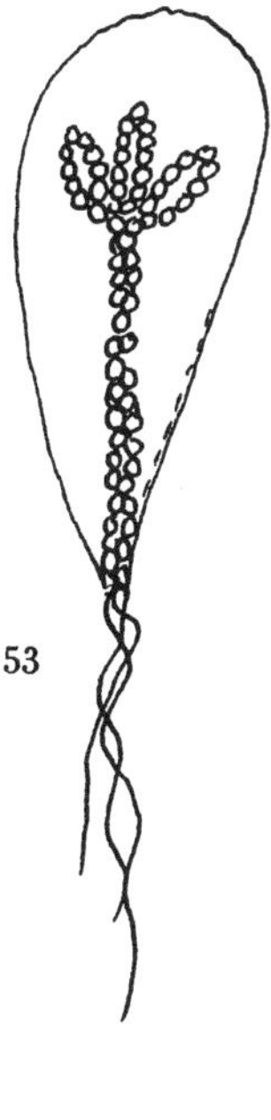

Fig. 53

Stalk—9″ high.

IVY

This pattern will make one 12″ sprig of ivy (HEDERA HELIX). It may be increased or decreased as desired. All of the leaves are made in the same way; however, the sizes vary.

Materials

Leaves, 1 bunch green beads for a 12″ sprig
Wires, 26- or 28-gauge for leaves; one 12″ piece of 16-gauge for stem.

Leaves

In order to emulate the shape of an ivy leaf it is necessary to form a frame with the 2nd and 3rd rows. Form the basic as for all other leaves. Before executing the next row, bend the beaded wire downward and form a narrow loop. Don't *make* a loop, merely *form* it. *Fig. 54.* Bring the beaded wire to the top of the basic, making a pointed top. Bring the beaded wire down the right side of the basic beads and *form* a matching downward loop on the right. Now you have your "frame." Work around the "frame" for the required number of rows, cut open the basic loop at the bottom of the loop, twist the wires together and tape them.

Unit 1. Basic: 8 beads, 5 rows. Make 3.

Unit 2. Basic: 12 beads, 5 rows. Make 2.

Unit 3. Basic: 12 beads, 7 rows. Make 2.

Unit 4. Basic: 14 beads, 7 rows. Make 2.

Unit 5. Basic: 16 beads, 9 rows. Make 4.

Assembly of Sprig

Tape a 12″ piece of 16-gauge stem wire. To the top of the stem wire, tape one small leaf. Tape down the stem wire for ¾″ and add another small leaf. Continue adding leaves to the stem wire, setting them about ¾″ apart. Allow ½″ of stem on the smaller leaves, and gradually increase the length to 1½″ on the larger leaves. Shape as in photo.

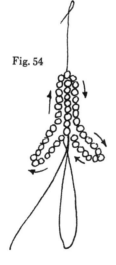

Fig. 54

Flower—2½" high, 2½" wide;
cluster—8" high, 5" wide.

LADY'S SLIPPER

The showy lady's slipper (CYPRIPEDIUM REGINAE), in the orchid family, is made in 3 units, and looks best done in pastel colors, or white with pale colors for contrast. They are an airy cluster of 3 flowers and 7 leaves to a bunch. Stemmed individually, they can be mounted on pins to wear as a corsage, or on an evening bag for accent. The flowers and leaves are stemmed separately, and when grouped together, are set at different levels. The stems of both flowers and leaves may be beaded with the large green stem beads on 19-gauge wire, or may be taped on 16-, 18-, or 19-gauge wires.

Materials

Flower, 2 colors—2 strands each for each flower
Leaves, ½ bunch green beads
Wires, 26- or 28-gauge for petals and leaves; 19-gauge for beaded stems; 18-gauge for taped stems; large green stem beads (optional)

Flower

Unit 1. BASIC: ⅞", pointed tops, round bottoms, 5 rows. Make 3 for each flower in color 1.

Unit 2. BASIC: ⅞", pointed tops, round bottoms, 3 rows. Make 2 for each flower in color 2.

Reduce the number of wires on each petal to 2 by cutting open the basic loop at the base of the petal.

Centers

Unit 1. Make 6 continuous single loops, measuring 1″ of beads for each loop. Make 1 for each flower in color 1.

Unit 2. Make 6 continuous single loops, measuring 1¼″ of beads for each loop. Make 1 for each flower in color 2.

Lip Petal (like sweet peas)

Make a basic loop with no beads on the basic. On the left side of the twisted wires, *form* a narrowed, horizontal loop, using 10 beads to form the loop. Start the loop at the bottom and bring it to the top. *Fig. 55.* Wrap the beading wire around the top basic wire, crossing in front, as always. On the right side of the twisted wires, and directly opposite the first loop, *form* another narrowed, horizontal loop, using 10 more beads for this loop. Wrap the beading wire around the bottom basic loop, crossing over the front of it, as always. Bead around this "frame," wrapping, top and bottom, as for any other petal or leaf. By forming these two 10-bead loops, you have created a horizontal basic. Continue wrapping beads around the frame until you have 5 rows of beads on each side (10 rows in all). Reduce the bottom wires to 2 by cutting open the basic loop at the bottom of the petal. Trim off top basic wires on all petals, as usual. Make 1 for each flower in color 1.

Fig. 55

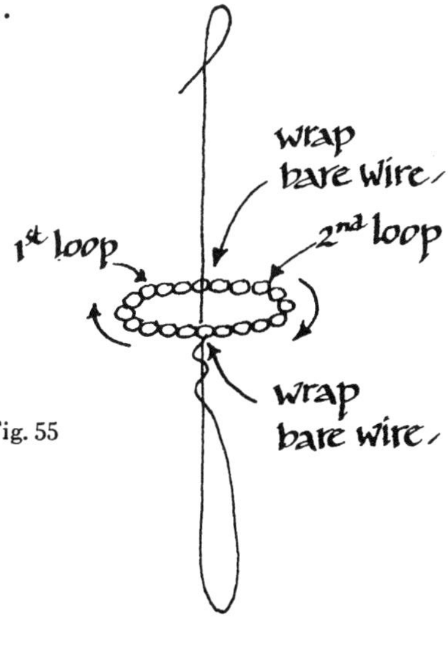

wrap bare wire

1ˢᵗ loop   2ⁿᵈ loop

wrap bare wire

Leaves

BASIC: ⅝″, pointed tops, pointed bottoms, 11 rows. Make 7 in green. Reduce the bottom wires of the leaves to 2, by cutting open the bottom basic loop at the base of the leaves, and tape the stems. Cut 7 19-gauge wires at odd lengths—between 7 and 9″. Bend down one end of each wire for ⅔″. Use a long-nosed pliers to form a narrow hook. Hook one wire into the base of each leaf and tape. *Fig. 56.* Cut off all but ⅔″ of the leaf wires. String small green beads onto 30- or 32-gauge wire, attach the open end of this wire to the base of the leaf and cover the tape with beads by wrapping the beads around and around the taped portion only. When the tape is covered with beads, wrap bare wire around the bare stem wire, and cut it off close, taking care not to cut the stem wire. Onto the bare stem wire (19-gauge) slip several inches of large green stem beads. Vary the lengths so that they will not be even in length. Make 3 with 3½″ of beads, 3 with 4″ of beads, and 1 with 5″ of beads. Tape the remaining stem wire, and include the last two beads as you tape. This will keep the stems from turning, and the beads from slipping. If you are not using the large green stem beads, cover the stem wires with tape.

Assembly of Flower

Combine the wires of the large petals (Unit 1, color 1) so that the center petal is slightly higher than the other two. *Fig. 57.* Twist the wires together. Attach a 15″ piece of assembly wire to the base of these three petals by wrapping it around twice, tightly. Combine the 2 center units by placing the small unit inside the large unit, and twisting the wires together. Set the center units at the base of the 3 petals, and combine them by wrapping the assembly wire around them, twice, tightly. Combine the 2 small petals by setting them together, face to face, right sides in, and twisting their wires together. Open them like wings, so that they are horizontal, and add them to the base of the units that are already combined, by wrapping them tightly with the assembly wire. Shape the horizontal lip petal by pressing the wrong side of the rib (basic wires) out, and the loops up and out (fold in half, right side in, then flair out the outer edges).

Attach the lip petal to the other units at the base of the wing petals, right side up, and wrap again with the assembly wire. Bend the lip petal forward and down. Cut a 10″ piece of 19-gauge wire for each flower, and bend ⅔″ of one end on all three of them. Catch the hooked end through a wire or two at the base of a flower. Pinch it closed with a plier and tape the wires for ⅔″. Cut off all other flower wires that might reach below the tape. Cover the taped part of the stems with small green beads that have been strung on assembly wire, just as you did for the leaves. Put 5½″ of stem beads onto the stems of two flowers, and 6″ of beads on the third one. Tape the remaining stem wires below the beads and include the two bottom beads in the taping. If you are not using stem beads, cover the entire stem with tape.

Assembly of Cluster

If the stems are beaded, gather together the flowers and tape them at the base of the stem beads. Tape on the leaves, one at a time, also at the base of the stem beads. If all the stems are taped, tape the flowers and leaves together, one at a time, so that they are at uneven lengths. Cut off stem wires to desired lengths for potting.

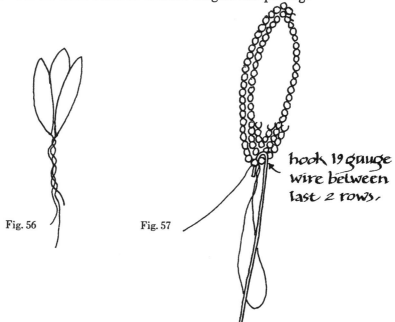

hook 19 gauge wire between last 2 rows.

Fig. 56   Fig. 57

Head—5½" long, 2¾" wide.
See also Plate V.

LILAC

Lilacs (Syringas) are limited in color to white, pale mauve, and lavenders shading to deep purple. They combine well with all spring flowers, but are beautiful all by themselves.

Materials

Buds and flowers, 1½ bunches beads in color
Leaves, 1 bunch green beads
Wires, 30-gauge for flowers; 26- or 28-gauge wire for leaves; 16-gauge wire for master stem

Flowers

All loops are made with 10 beads each, and all stems are double beaded for ¾". The loops and the stems are in the flower color.

Two inches from the open end of the spool wire, make 4 continuous single loops using 10 beads for each loop. After completing the fourth loop, allow 2" of bare spool wire, and cut the flower from the spool. Twist the wires of the flower together twice—close to the base of the flower. Onto both wires, feed ¾" of beads, using the same color bead as you used for the 4 loops. Push these beads close to the base of the 4 loops and twist the wires together. Make 78 flowers in all. Cut the tape in half, lengthwise, stretch, and individually tape the stems of all 78 flowers. *Fig. 58.*

Buds

Three inches from the open end of the spool wire, make a 10-bead loop. Bead up the front and down the back of the loop. Twist the 2 wires together, twice, close to the base of the loop. Allow 3" of bare spool wire at the base of the loop, and cut the bud from the spool. Onto both wires, feed ¾" of beads. Push the beads close to the base of the bud, and twist both wires together. Make 28 buds in all. Tape all bud stems with half-width tape—the same as for the flowers. *Fig. 59.*

Leaves

Small. BASIC: 6 beads, pointed tops, round bottoms, 9 rows. Make 4 in green.

Large. BASIC: 6 beads, pointed tops, round bottoms, 11 rows. Make 8 in green.

Tape all leaves individually.

Assembly of Flowers

The flowers and buds are combined into units of various sizes.

Unit 1. Tape together the stems of 4 buds, using half-width tape. Make 1.

Unit 2. Tape together the stems of 1 bud and 3 flowers. *Fig. 60.* Make 3.

Unit 3. Tape together the stems of 3 flowers. *Fig. 61.* Make 7.

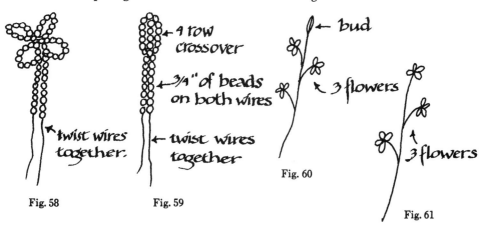

Fig. 58

Fig. 59

Fig. 60

Fig. 61

Unit 4. Tape together the stems of 2 buds and 3 flowers. *Fig. 62.* Make 6.

Unit 5. Tape together the stems of 3 buds and 5 flowers. *Fig. 63.* Make 3.

Unit 6. Tape together the stems of 5 flowers. *Fig. 64.* Make 3.
When combining the units, add the flowers one at a time, setting each one ⅓" below the preceding ones, so as to elongate each sprig.

Stemming of Flowers

Cut a 10" piece of 16-gauge wire and tape it. Tape Unit 1—the 4 combined buds—to the top of the 16-gauge wire, no bud stem showing. Tape down the stem wire for 1" and add the 3 sprigs of Unit 2 around the stem. Continue with the remaining units, taping them around the stem. Continue adding the remaining units, taping them around and down the stem.

Stemming of Leaves

Cut 2 pieces of 18-gauge wire 8" long, and tape them. To the top of one 18-gauge wire, tape 2 small leaves, allowing ½" of leaf stem to show. Tape down the heavy stem wire for 1" and tape on 1 large leaf—on the left side of the heavy stem wire. Continue taping for 1" and add another large leaf on the right. Add 2 more large leaves, 1" apart, one on the left and one on the right. Do the same to the other 8" piece of 18-gauge wire. Mount 1 spray of leaves to the left side of the flower stem and another to the right side, placing the second one about 1½" lower than the first one.

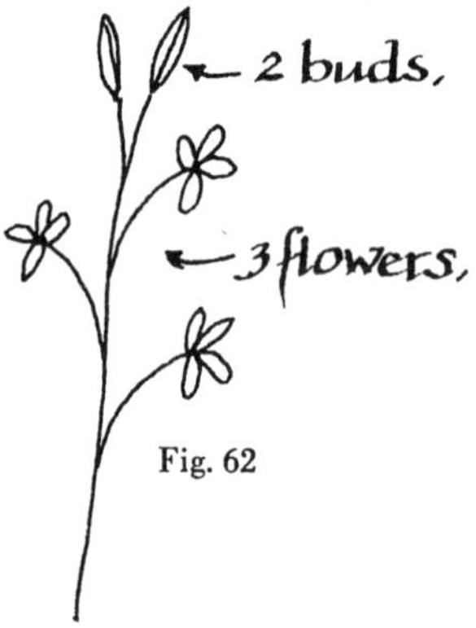

2 buds,

3 flowers.

Fig. 62

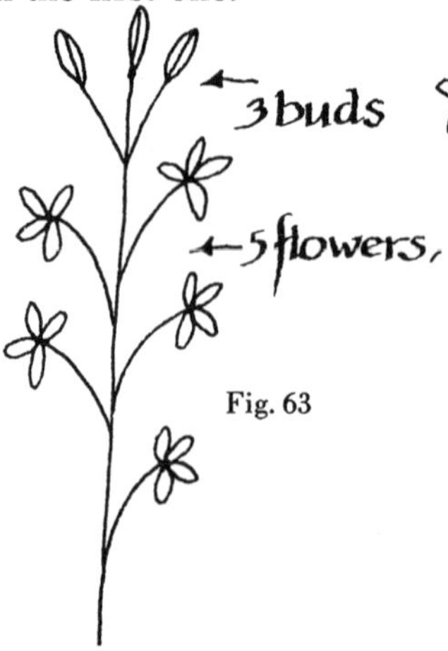

3 buds

5 flowers,

Fig. 63

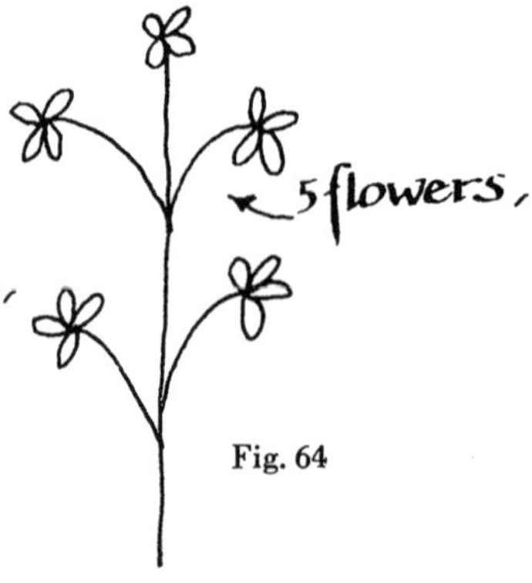

5 flowers,

Fig. 64

Cluster—7" high,
7" wide.

LILY-of-the-VALLEY

CONVALLARIA of the lily family is noted for its white, nodding flowers. The pattern described here is for a cluster of flowers and leaves. Two are sufficient for one small container; however, one cluster can be divided and used in a mixed floral arrangement.

Materials

Flowers, 1 bunch white beads
Leaves, 1 bunch green beads
Wires, 18- or 19-gauge for stems and bracing leaves; 26- or 28-gauge wire for making leaves, 28- or 30-gauge wire for making flowers.

Flowers

This count is for 1 sprig of flowers only. Make 4 sprigs for each cluster.

Unit 1. Make 1 10-bead loop. Make 1.

Unit 2. Make 3 continuous single loops using 12 beads for each loop. Make 2.

Unit 3. Make 4 continuous single loops, using 14 beads for each loop. Make 3.

Unit 4. Make 4 continuous single loops, using 16 beads for each loop. Make 2.

Unit 5. Make 5 continuous single loops, using 20 beads for each loop. Make 5.

Narrow the loops on all flowers and shape the loops out at the bottom and in at the top to form a ball. Twist the stem wires together and cut off all but 2″ of the stem. Use half width tape for the flower stems, by cutting the tape in half, lengthwise and then stretching it.

Leaves

Small. BASIC: 1¾″, pointed tops, pointed bottoms, 19 rows. Make 2.

Large. BASIC: 2¼″, pointed tops, pointed bottoms, 19 rows. Make 2.

Reinforce these leaves by bracing them with an 8″ piece of taped 18- or 19-gauge wire. Cut off all but 1″ of the top basic wire on each leaf. Cover this 1″ of wire with tape. To the top of each leaf, tape a piece of bracing wire. Bring the bracing wire down the back of the leaf and tape it to the bottom wires of the leaf. Lace each leaf in 3 places— ⅓ of the way down from the top, ⅓ of the way up from the bottom, and once through the middle, including the bracing wires as you lace. Combine the stems of the 2 large leaves and tape the stems together so that the bottoms of the leaves are even. To the left side of this pair of leaves tape a small leaf. To the right side, tape the other small leaf.

Assembly of Flower Sprigs

Cut 4 pieces of 18- or 19-gauge wire approximately 8″ long and tape them individually. Tape on the bell flowers to the stem wire. Allow ½″ of stem showing on each flower. Start with the small flowers at the top (Unit 1 and 2), then continue with 3, 4, 5, and 6. When you have assembled all 4 sprigs, line up the stem wires so that they are even at the bottom, and tape all 4 stems together just below the bottom flowers. Combine the flowers and leaves by placing the leaves behind the flowers and taping the stems together.

1   2   3   4   5

Flower—1¼″ wide; leaf—2¼″
long; spray—10″ high.
See also Plate VI.

MARIGOLD

This marigold is a small but vibrant flower. Its colors run toward the yellows, oranges and browns. This pattern calls for two-toned ones, but they can be made in solid yellow or solid orange. As you work on the units for the flower, keep your loops very close together, and tuck each new loop that you make slightly under the preceding one.

Materials

Flower, 1½ strands of yellow and 1 strand orange for each flower
  or 1½ strands of orange and 1 strand brown for each flower
Leaves, less than 1 strand green for each leaf
Wires, 28- or 30-gauge for flower; 26- or 28-gauge for leaf; 18-gauge for stem

Flowers

Unit 1. Make 20 continuous single loops, measuring 1″ of beads for each one. Close the unit into a circle and twist the wires together. Make 1 for each flower.

Unit 2. Make 18 continuous single loops, measuring ¾″ of heads for each one. Close the unit into a circle and twist the wires together. Make 1 for each flower.

Unit 3. Make 12 continuous single loops, measuring 12 beads for each one. Do *not* close this unit. Make 1 for each flower.

Unit 4. Make 3 continuous loops, measuring 8 beads for each one. Close the loops by twisting the wires together. Make 1 for each flower.

Assembly of Flowers

Set Unit 4 into Unit 3 and twist both sets of wires together. Set Units 4 and 3 in the center of Unit 2 and twist all wires together. Set Units 4, 3 and 2 in the center of Unit 1 and twist all wires togeher. Tape the wires.

Leaves (in green)

String at least 14" of green beads for each leaf. Three inches from the open end of the wire, make a narrow loop of 1¼" of beads. Push 8 beads to the base of the loop. Close to these 8 beads, make another narrow loop of 1¼" of beads. Push 8 beads to the base of the second loop and close to the 8 beads make a third loop of 1¼" of beads. Continue unil you have 9 loops separated by 8 beads. *Fig. 65.* Allow 3" mcre of bare wire at the end of the ninth loop and cut the leaf from the spool. Fold the string of loops in half and twist the wires together. Open the fold. Put a half twist in between each pair of loops and bend loop up and out, rather sharply. *Fig. 66.*

Assembly of Flowers and Leaves

You may combine 1 flower and 3 leaves or 2 flowers and 4 leaves on a 6 or 7" piece of·18-gauge wire that has been taped. Tape a leaf at the top, then a flower and a leaf. There should be no stem showing on the leaves, but 1½" of stem on the flowers. Space the flowers and leaves ¾" apart.

Fig. 65

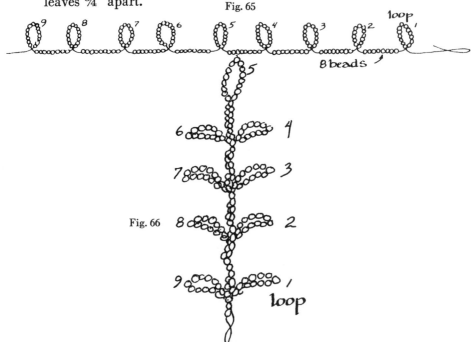

Fig. 66

loop

Flower—2" wide; cluster—7" wide.
See also Plate I, IX.

MORNING GLORIES

The morning glory (IPOMOEA) is great fun to make. It's a challenge because an entirely new technique is involved. The flower is worked on a wire frame, using 24-gauge wire. The beads with which the flower is actually made are strung on 30- or 32-gauge wire. The flower can be very easily shaded in 2 or 3 different tones of the same color, by anticipating the amount of wire needed to complete the flower (usually about a yard) and feeding onto this extended wire the amount of beads to achieve the desired shading. The flower has 12 rows of beads in all. If you wish to make the flower in three colors, work the first 6 rows in the first color, feed on enough beads in the second color to work the next 3 rows, then change the color again and work the last 3 rows. If you wish to work in 2 colors only, execute the first 9 rows in color 1, then edge the flower with the last 3 rows in a contrast color. Their natural colorings are white, white and yellow, blue, blue and white, lavender, lavender and purple, fuchsia and white, and pale pink tipped with darker pink. The multi-shaded ones are usually white at the bottom, and gradually grow deeper in tone at the top; stamens are usually yellow.

Flower

Cut 6 pieces of 24-gauge wire 4" long. Stack them so that they are even at the bottom. Twist the wires together for ¾" very tightly. If you use 2 pliers, the twisting will be tighter and much easier. Open out the untwisted section of wires to resemble the spoke of an umbrella. *Fig. 67.* Keep the spokes horizontal to the twisted ones. The shaping of the flower is done after it is completed. String your beads on assembly wire (30- or 32-gauge). Attach the open end of this wire to the twisted wires, and at the base of the spokes. Wrap the wire securely, 2 or 3 times. These ribs (spokes) are going to be treated as though they are basic wires without the basic beads on them. Therefore, you will cross over the top of each spoke as you wrap the beading wire. Start by wrapping bare beading wire around any one of the ribs, once. Work from the center, out. Slide 2 beads between spoke 1 and spoke 2. Wrap the beading wire around spoke 2. Slide 2 beads between spoke 2 and spoke 3, and wrap the beading wire around spoke 3. Continue putting 2 beads between each spoke, wrapping the bead wire over the top and around each spoke as you work to complete row 1. Continue as before, but put 3 beads in between each spoke, thus completing row 2. Continue on to the third row by putting 4 beads in between each spoke, making them fit. Keep the rows of beads and the beads themselves close together. After the third row has been completed, it is not necesary to count the number of beads between each rib. Put in whatever it takes to fill the space between the spokes. Keep the spokes as straight as possible and evenly spaced. Continue until you have completed 12 rows of beads. To finish off the flower, bring bare bead wire down the back of the last spoke that was wrapped, wrap the bead wire around the twisted wires of the frame and cut the wire from the spool. Cut off all but ¼" of wire from each spoke, and bend them back to the wrong side of the flower. To

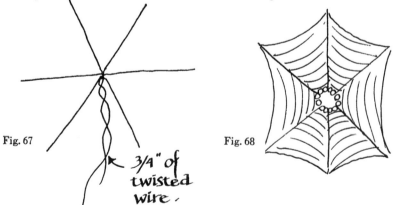

Fig. 67

3/4" of twisted wire.

Fig. 68

shape the flower, press the spokes out and the rows of beads in. *Fig. 68.* Make 4.

Stamen

You need a darning needle and 4" of beads strung on 30- or 32-gauge wire to make the stamens. Wrap the open end of the wire around the pointed end of the needle for three wraps. Remove the needle from the little coil of wire, and trim off the straight wire very close to the coil. Push 1" of beads up to the coil. At the bottom of the 1" of beads, make a basic loop. Make the loop tight, so that the 1" of beads is firm between the coiled wire and the basic loop. Measure another 1" of beads, and push them down to the basic loop. At the other end of this second 1" of beads, make another coil of wire by wrapping the wire around the point of the needle, but wrap 6 times. Repeat with another 1" of beads, another basic loop, another 1" of beads, and another coil around the needle 3 times. Cut the stamen from the spool of wire close to the top of the last coil in the wire. Cut open the basic loops at the bottom of the loops. Cut in the middle of the 6 coils of wire, and combine the two units by twisting the bottom wires together. Insert the stamen wires into the center of the flower and twist the wires together at the base of the flower. Cut off any stamen wires that might be longer than the flower wires, and cover the wires with tape. Make 1 for each flower. *Fig. 69.*

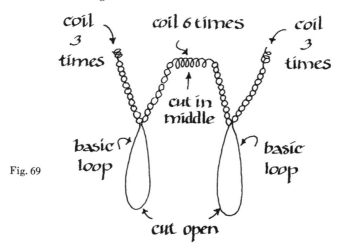

Fig. 69

Morning glories are particularly attractive when their stems are beaded with the large green stem beads, so use them if they are available to you. However, these beads will fit only on 19-gauge wire. In either case, whether you use the green stem beads or cover the stem wires with tape, the assembly is much the same. Both will be explained. If you are not using the stem beads, mount the flowers and leaves on 18-gauge wire.

Assembly of Flower

Cut 10" pieces of 18- or 19-gauge wire for the flower. With a long-nosed pliers, make a sharp bend at one end of one wire. Hook the bent end of the wire into 1 of the flower spokes, at the base of the flower. Cover the hooked wire and flower wires with tape to secure tightly and cut away all but ¾" of the flower wires. Thread onto 30- or 32-gauge wire enough small green beads to cover the taped part of the stem by wrapping the open end of the beading wire around the base of the flower tightly, then wrapping the strung beads around the stem until the taped part is covered with beads. To finish it off, wrap the fine wire around the bare stem wire very tightly 3 or 4 times, then cut away the fine wire very close to the stem. At this point, if you are using stem beads, slip onto the flower stem 7" of the large green beads. Push them up close to the base of the flower, and using a *round* pencil, coil the stem around the pencil until all of the stem beads are coiled. Cover the remaining stem wire with tape, and include the last 2 stem beads when you tape. This will prevent the beads from slipping and the stem from turning about. If you are not using the stem beads, cover the stem wire with tape, then coil the stem around the pencil.

Leaves

BASIC: ¾", pointed tops, round bottoms, 11 rows. Make 12. Tape the stems on all the leaves, then, by taping them together, make 4 groupings of 3 leaves each. *Fig. 70.* Set the center leaf ⅓" above the other 2. Cut one 8" piece of 18- or 19-gauge wire for each grouping of 3 leaves (4 in all). Put a sharp bend in one end of the wire, as you did for the flower, and hook the bend into the taped leaf wires. Cover the hook with tape, and cut away all but ¾" of the leaf stems. If you are using the stem beads, cover the taped wire with small beads—just as you did for the flowers—then slide onto the 19-gauge stem wire 2¼" of green stem beads and tape the stem, including the 2 bottom beads when you tape. If you are not using the stem beads, merely cover the stem wire with tape. Do not coil the leaf stems.

Combining Flowers and Leaves

If the stems of all flowers and leaves are beaded, gather all stem wires together at the base of the beading and tape them together, securely. Cut off excess stem wires to desired lengths for potting. If the stems are just taped, gather the stems of the flowers together at the bottom of the coils. Allow 2½" of stem on the leaf groupings, and add them to the flower stems, all at the same place. Cut off wires to desired lengths for potting.

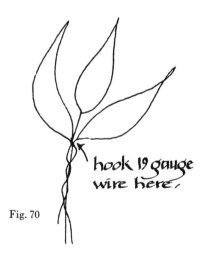

hook 19 gauge wire here,

Fig. 70

1	2	3	4	5

6" long, 5" wide.
See also Plate I.

ORCHID

There are thousands of species of orchids in many sizes and color combinations. This pattern was created to execute the one with which we are most familiar—the genus Cattleya—and is most effective in two shades of lavender or in white and yellow.

Materials

Petals and Centers, 1 bunch
Throat, ½ bunch in a contrast color
Wire, 26- or 28-gauge wire.

Petals

Unit 1. BASIC: 1½", very pointed tops, round bottoms, 15 rows. Make 2 in lavender or white.

Unit 2. BASIC: 1¾" very pointed tops, round bottoms, 7 rows. Make 2 in lavender or white.

Unit 3. BASIC: 2¼", very pointed tops, round bottoms, 9 rows. Make 1 in lavender or white.

Throat

Make the throat in 2 parts, as it will be much easier. The loops are continuous single loops formed as close together as possible. Leave 3" of spool wire before making first loop.

Unit 1. Measure 2½" of beads and form loop 1. Measure 3" of beads and form loop 2. Measure 3½" of beads and form loop 3. Measure 4¼" of beads and form loop 4. Measure 5" of beads and form loop 5. Measure 5¾" of beads and form loop 6. Measure 6¼" of beads and form loop 7. Measure 7" of beads and form loop 8. Leave 3" of spool wire at the end of the 8th loop and cut the unit from the spool.

Unit 2. Leave 3" of bare spool wire. Measure 6¼" of beads and remake loop 7. Measure 5¾" of beads and remake loop 6. Measure 5" of beads and remake loop 5. Measure 4¼" of beads and remake loop 4. Measure 3½" of beads and remake loop 3. Measure 3" of beads and remake loop 2. Measure 2½" of beads and remake loop 1. Take notice of the fact that you have made only *one* loop 8 when you made Unit 1.

Combine Units 1 and 2 by twisting together the wires at the base of the last loop of Unit 1 and the first loop of Unit 2. Leave 3" of bare spool wire at the end of Unit 2 and cut the wire from the spool. Lace the loops together in 2 places—first, one-half of the way up from the bottom, and then one-third of the way down from the top. *Fig. 71.* Use the skip lace method as for Daffodil crowns, Canterbury Bells, Bells of Ireland, etc. After lacing, combine the wire at the base of loop 1 in Unit 1 to the wire at the base of the last loop in Unit 2 and twist them together.

Stamen

Make 3 continuous single loops, measuring 3″ of beads for each loop. Twist the wires together, and cut from spool. Narrow the loops and twist them together. Insert the stamen into the throat and twist together both sets of wires. Shape the throat like a cone and flare out the loops at the top.

Attach a 15″ piece of assembly wire to the base of the throat. Add, one at a time, the petals of the flower, all around the base of the throat. Place them as in photo and cover the wires with tape.

Fig. 71

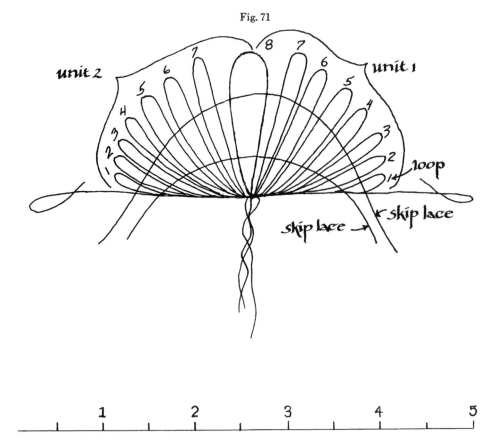

Flower—2¾" wide; leaf group—2½" wide.
See also Plate VI.

ORIENTAL POPPIES

When one thinks of a poppy (PAPAVER ORIENTALIS), the color that first comes to mind is usually red. However, oriental poppies grow not only in bright Chinese red, but also in orange, yellow, violet, and white. No matter what color you decide on, they are a very showy flower. They have a proud and graceful head with an abundance of green leaves on a heavy stem. The centers may be made in either black or brown.

Materials

Petals, 1 strand for each petal
Leaves, 1 bunch
Wires, 16-gauge for stem; 26- or 28-gauge for all parts; 30- or 32-gauge for assembly

Petals

BASIC: ½", round tops, pointed bottoms, 13 rows. Make 8 for each flower.

Centers

Unit 1. 3 continuous single loops using 1" of beads.

Unit 2. 12 continuous single loops using 1½" of beads in contrasting color for each loop.

Calyx

12 continuous loops using 2" of beads for each loop. Keep these loops

oval at the top and narrow at the bottom. Close the loops by twisting the bare wires together. Do not tape. Make 1 for each flower, in green.

Leaves

BASIC: 1½", pointed tops, round bottoms, 5 rows. Make 15 for each flower in green and tape the stems. Cut the tape in half, then stretch so that the stems will be slim. Combine the leaves into 3 groups of 5 leaves each as shown in *Fig. 72* staggering them in height.

Assembly of Flowers

Combine the centers by closing both Units 1 and Units 2. Insert Unit 1 into Unit 2 and twist the 2 sets of wires together. Cover 1" of these wires with tape. Tape a 10" piece of 16-gauge wire, and directly on top of this wire, tape the combined center units. Cut a piece of 30- or 32-gauge wire and wrap one end of it around the base of the center units, twice, tightly. Add the flower petals, one at a time, right side up, wrapping with the assembly wire with each addition. Add 4 petals, opposite one another, then add the remaining 4 setting them in between the first 4. Thin out the wires by cutting them off at odd lengths, and cover them with tape. Close the wires of the calyx and insert the flower stem into the middle of the loops. Push the calyx up to the base of the flower and arrange the loop evenly around the petals. Cover the calyx wires with tape, cup the flower petals up and inward. Cup the center loops inward. Bend the flower head forward. Four-and-one half inches below the base of the flower, tape on the first grouping of 5 leaves—on the left side of the master stem. One-half inch lower tape on the second group of 5 leaves—on the right side. One inch lower, tape on the third set of 5 leaves—in the front. If you are using several poppies in an arrangement and 1 or 2 of them will be set low in the container, the lower ones will not necessarily need the full complement of leaves. Ten should be sufficient.

Fig. 72

Flower—1½″ long, 1¼″
wide; cluster—3½″ high, 4″ wide.

PANSY (WILD)

There are 4 flowers, 1 bud, and 6 leaves to the bunch. Their natural colors are lavender, blue, yellow, and white.

Materials

Petals, ½ bunch of beads
Centers, ½ strand
Leaves, ½ bunch of green beads
*Wires, 28- or 30-gauge for flowers and leaves, or 26-gauge brass wire
    if desired; 16-gauge for master stem*

Petals

Large. There are 2 large petals to each flower, but they are made as 1 unit, because they are continuous wraparound loops. The count is one 8-bead loop, wrapped around 3 times—make 2—all in one.

Start with 5″ of bare wire, make an 8-bead loop. Wrap beads around the 8-bead loop 3 times, giving the petal 3 more rows (4 in all), fastening each row by wrapping beading wire around the beginning wire at the base of the original 8-bead loop each time you encircle the loops with beads. Now, to the left of this wrapped loop, make another 8-bead loop, leaving ¼″ of wire between the wrapped loop and the new 8-bead loop. *Fig. 73.* Encircle the second

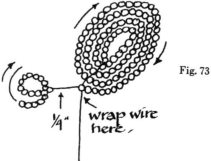

Fig. 73

¼″   wrap wire here

107

8-bead loop with beads, 3 times. Allow 5″ of bare spool wire at the base of the petal, and cut the petals from the spool. Twist the bottom wires together, 3 or 4 times close to the base of the petals. Make 1 unit for each flower.

Small. The small petal is made in the same way as the large one except for a change in count. Make an 8-bead loop 5″ from the end of the spool wire, and encircle this loop twice, with beads (3 rows in all). Make a second 8-bead loop ¼″ to the left, and encircle it twice with beads. Allow 5″ of bare spool wire and cut the petals from the spool. Make 1 unit for each flower.

Lip Petal. Five inches from the end of the wire, make a loop of 14 beads. Twist the wires together 2 or 3 times. Shape this loop horizontally. *Fig. 74.* Wrap around this flattened loop 3 times, with beads. Allow 5″ of bare spool wire, and cut the petal from the spool. Make 1 for each flower.

Stamen

Make one 8-bead loop in a contrast color. Make 1 for each flower.

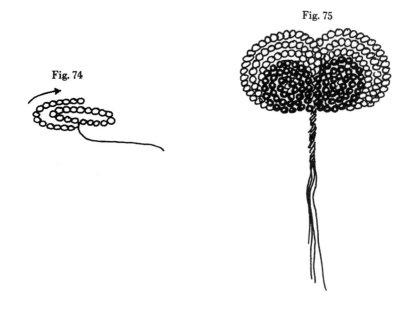

Fig. 75

Fig. 74

Assembly of Flowers

Place a unit of small petals on top of a unit of large petals so that the bottoms are even, and twist both sets of wires together for an inch or so. *Fig. 75.* Attach the stamen to the base of the lip petal, on the right side. Twist their wires together. Join the lip petal and stamen to the combined set of large and small petals by placing them face to face —right sides in—bottoms even—and twist all wires together to form the flower stem. Cover the wires with half width tape. Open the flower by bending the lip petal forward and down. Pinch the lip petal vertically, then curve the edges up and out.

Leaves

BASIC: 8 beads, round tops, very pointed bottoms, 9 rows. Make 6. Open the basic loop at the bottom of the loop so that you have 3 wires at the bottom of each leaf when finished. Tape the leaves individually with half width tape the full length of the wires.

Bud

The bud consists of 1 large petal—one 8-bead loop plus 3 wraps, times 2. Cup the 2 petals, wrong side in, and tape the wires. Make 1 for each cluster. Tape with half width tape.

Assembly of Cluster

Tape a piece of 16-gauge wire about 4 or 5″ long. Add the flowers, bud, and leaves to the top of the 16-gauge wire, varying the lengths of the stems of the flowers and leaves.

These flower clusters blend extremely well with Lily-of-the-Valley for an all white and green arrangement.

Branch—11″ long.

PHILODENDRON

Materials

Leaves, 1 bunch green beads
Wires, 26- or 28-gauge for leaves
 One 10″ piece of 16-gauge wire

Leaves

All leaves have pointed tops and round bottoms. The basic on all leaves is 6 beads. Make 2 leaves with 5 rows; make 2 leaves with 7 rows; make 2 leaves with 9 rows; make 3 leaves with 11 rows; make 2 leaves with 13 rows; make 3 leaves with 15 rows. Work with a long basic loop, about 8″, and curve the basic wire to the right as you make the leaves. (As for butterfly wing.) This pattern will make a 10″ sprig of philodendron. It may be increased or decreased as desired.

Cut open the basic loops at the bottoms of the loops and cover the wires with tape.

Assembly

Tape a 10″ piece of 16-gauge wire. To the top of it, tape 1 small leaf. Tape down the heavy stem wire for ¾″ and add another small leaf. Continue adding leaves to the heavy wire setting them about ¾″ apart. Allow ½″ of stem on the smaller sized leaves and gradually increase the length to 1½″.

110

Branch—12½″ long.
See also Plate VII.

PUSSY WILLOW

Pussy willow, genus SALIX, a charming accent to any grouping of Spring flowers, is particularly lovely when combined with forsythia and daffodils.

Materials

Pussy willows, ½ bunch gray beads
Calyx, 2 or 3 strings brown beads
Wires, 28- or 30-gauge for pussy willows; 16-gauge stem wire
Stems, brown or twig tape

Pussy Willows

Three inches from the open end of the spool wire, make a narrow loop of 1″ of beads. Encircle this loop with beads, and wrap the spool wire around the starting wire. Directly next to this, make another narrow loop of 1″ of beads and encircle it with beads. Twist the bottom wires together. *Fig. 76.* Make 20 for sprig.

Fig. 76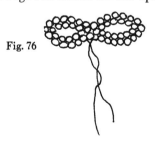

Calyx

Make 2 continuous single loops, using 12 beads for each loop and twist the wires together, twice, tightly, at the base of the loops. Make 1 for each pussy willow in brown.

Assembly of Pussy Willows and Calyx

Cup the pussy willow units, wrong side in, and set the bottom of each pussy willow unit into a calyx. Form the calyx units so that they embrace the bottom of the pussy willow. Twist the wires tightly together, and cover the wires with brown or twig tape that has been cut in half, lengthwise. Cut off all but 1½″ of the stem on each pussy willow.

Use taped 16-gauge wire for the master stem of the largest branch, and 18-gauge wire for the smaller twigs that are added to it. Don't show any stem on the pussy willow itself. They should be flush to the master stem. There is no set pattern for building branches. Merely start with a heavy branch, and add small sprigs wherever you wish *Fig. 77.*

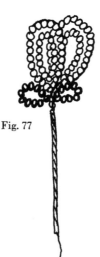

Fig. 77

Flower—¾″ wide; cluster—3½″ wide,
with leaves—4½″ wide.

QUEEN ANNE'S LACE

This wildling, with its filmy white blooms that mature in summer, is a flower arranger's favorite. A member of the carrot family, its botanical name is DAUCUS CAROTA.

Materials

Flowers, 7 strands beads for 20 flowers
Centers, 40 beads in a contrast color for 20 flowers
Leaves, ½ bunch green beads
Wires, 6″ piece of 16- or 18-gauge for stem; 26- or 28-gauge for flowers and leaves

Flower

Make 5 continuous single loops using 12 beads for each loop. Leave 4″ of spool wire at the beginning and at the end. Make the center part of the flower by bringing the end wire under loop 1 and up between loops 1 and 2. Put onto this wire 2 beads of a contrast color. Cross the wire over the center of the flower and down between loops 4 and 5. Twist the 2 wires together. Cut tape in half and tape the stems of the flowers. Make 20 for each head.

Leaves

BASIC: ½″, pointed tops, round bottoms, 15 rows. Make 4 to a head. Cut open basic loop at the bottom of the loop and tape the wires.

Assembly

Cut and tape a 6 or 7″ piece of 16- or 18-gauge wire. Allowing 2½″ of stem on each flower, tape the flowers to the top of the heavy stem wire—all at the same level—to form a ball of flowers. Tape the leaves all around the stem—right side up—one at a time, allowing 1″ of leaf stem. Continue taping to the bottom of the heavy stem wire. Bend the flower head forward and slightly curl the leaves.

113

Flower—3″ wide; leaf—2½″ long, 1½″ wide.
See also Plate IV, IX.

ROSE OF SHARON

The rose of Sharon (ALTHAEA) normally grows in bush form, and its colors are both subtle and vibrant. Solid white ones with bright red or fuchsia stamens are extremely attractive. Pale blues, lavenders, and pinks are typical of Nature's own colorings too. The flowers and leaves can be mounted either singly with 3 leaves, or in pairs with 4 or 5 leaves. The leaves are made the same way as the leaves for Chrysanthemum, except for a change in the measurement of the Basic.

Materials

Flower, 5 strands beads

Stamen, 1 strand contrast color

Leaves, ½ bunch green beads

Wires, 1 8″ piece of 16-gauge wire for stem; 26- or 28-gauge for flowers and leaves

Petals

BASIC: 7 beads, round tops, pointed bottoms, 11 rows. Make 5 for each flower.

Stamen

BASIC: 2 beads, round top, round bottom. 8 rows. Make 1 for each flower.

Make the first 6 rows of the stamen in the same color bead as the petal. Allowing 6″ of bare spool wire at the end of the 6th row, cut the wire from the spool. (see Tipping, Edging, and Shading in the

General Instructions Chapter.) Feed onto this wire enough beads of a contrast color to complete rows 7 and 8. Because the pattern calls for an even number of rows, you will be finishing at the top of the unit—where the single basic wire is. Open the basic loop at the bottom of the loop. You now have 2 wires at the top and 2 wires at the bottom. String 22 beads of the contrast color onto the spool wire, and make a narrow loop with the 22 beads. Twist their wires together, spiral the loop of beads by giving it 2 half twists, and insert the spiraled loop wires into the center of the right side of the stamen. Join the end wires of the stamen to the loop wires, on the wrong side of the stamen, and twist them together.

Assembly of Flowers

Stack 5 petals—one on top of the other—right side up—so that the bottoms are even. Twist all petal wires together. Spread the petals into an open circle, and shape them up from the bottom and out at the top. Insert the stamen into the center of the flower by sliding it between 2 petals. Wrap the stamen wires around the petal wires, and cover the wires with tape.

Leaves

BASIC: 1¾", pointed tops, round bottoms, 3 rows.
Execute the above count, then make 2 loopbacks on either side of this count. Make the first loopback on the left. The top of it should reach to the top of the basic row. Make a second loopback on the right. Have it match the first loopback in height. The third loopback should be made on the left side, and reach to the middle of the basic row. Make the fourth loopback on the right. Have it match the third loopback in height. Twist the bottom wires together and open the basic loop at the bottom of the loop. Tape the stems.

Stemming Flowers and Leaves

Cut a piece of 16-gauge wire to the desired length, and tape it. To the top of this wire, tape a leaf. An inch or so below the leaf, tape a flower. Bend the head of the flower forward before taping it to the stem wire. Tape on the flowers and leaves in whatever pattern you desire. Groups of 2 or more flowers can be used as a spray for height or width, and groups of 3 can be used to fill in spaces around the bottom of a floral arrangement.

Large flower—3½" wide; medium
flower—2½" wide; small flower—
1½" wide. See also Plate VIII.

ROSE SPRAY

Roses are a universal favorite and when beaded they have extra
glamour. There are hybrids in practically every color. When you
make this rose spray, you learn not only the flower in 3 sizes, but
also how to stem each size. This spray consists of a bud, a medium
rose and a large, full-blown one.

Materials

Flowers, 2 bunches
Leaves, 1 bunch
Wires, 26- or 28-gauge for petals and leaves; 16-gauge for stems

Petals

All petals are round, top and bottom, and the basic count on all
petals is 6 beads. Reduce all bottom wires to 2, by cutting open the
bottom basic loop at the base of the petal.
Bud. Make 2 petals with 9 rows; make 2 petals with 11 rows.
Medium rose. Make 2 petals with 9 rows, 2 petals with 11 rows, and
4 petals with 15 rows.
Large rose. Make 2 petals with 9 rows, 2 petals with 11 rows, 4 petals

with 15 rows, and 5 petals with 19 rows. Lace individually the 19-row petals.

Sepals in Green Beads

BASIC: 10 beads, pointed tops, round bottoms, 5 rows. Make 14: 4 for bud and 5 each for the medium and large rose. Reduce the bottom wires to 2.

Leaves in Green Beads

Small. BASIC: 6 beads, pointed tops, round bottoms, 9 rows. Make 3. *Large.* BASIC: 6 beads, pointed tops, round bottoms, 11 rows. Make 8. Tape the leaf stems after opening the basic loop at the bottom of the loop.

Assembly of Flower

Make the bud first, by cupping the two 9-row petals, wrong side in, one locking into the other. Twist the bottom wires together. Cup two 11-row petals, right side in, then bend back the tips of the petals. To the base of the combined 9-row petals, wrap securely a piece of assembly wire, and add the two 11-row petals close to the base of the first 2. Add these 2 at the overlap of the first 2. Add, with the assembly wire, 4 sepals, wrong side in. Wrap the assembly wire around twice, tightly, with each addition. Cut off the excess assembly wire, and cover the remaining wires with tape.

Start the medium rose and the large rose in the same way, then adding for the medium rose the 4 petals with 15 rows, and for the large rose, adding the 4 petals with 15 rows and the 5 petals with 19 rows. Cup all petals before assembling. This will help in shaping your rose as you put it together. Add 5 sepals to the medium rose, and 5 sepals to the large rose. Add them, one at a time with the assembly wire, right sides in, then curl them outward and down. Tape the stem wires.

Assembly of Spray

Cut 3 pieces of 16-gauge wire—one 11" long, another 9" long, and the other 7" long. Tape all 3 individually. To the top of the 11" piece of wire tape a small leaf. Tape down the stem wire for 1½" and add a large leaf on the left side of the stem. Tape down 1" and add another large leaf. Tape down 1½" and tape on the bud. Bend the head of the bud forward.

At the top of the 9" piece of wire, add 3 leaves in the same way as for the bud. Two inches below the third leaf, tape on the medium rose, and bend its head forward.

At the top of the 7" piece of stem wire tape on 1 small leaf and 4 large leaves. Tape down 2½" and tape on the large rose. Bend the head of the rose forward.

Tape the bud stem and the medium rose stem together below the medium rose, then add the large rose stem about 2½" lower. Give the whole spray an "S" curve and turn down the sepals on the medium and large rose.

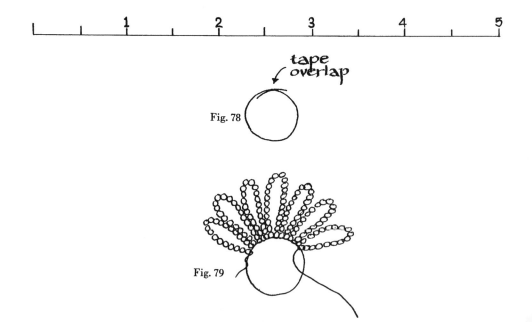

Fig. 78

tape
overlap

Fig. 79

Overall—9" high; flower—3" wide;
leaf—2¾" long, 1½" wide. See also Plate X.

SHASTA DAISY

CHRYSANTHEMUM MAXIMUM is chiefly grown in a large flowered hybrid form known as the Shasta daisy. Its leaves are long, narrow and toothed, but not deeply cut. Incidentally, chrysanthemum means golden flower in Greek.

Materials

Flower, 45" beads for each flower
Center, ½ strand in a contrast color
Leaves, 2½ strands green beads
Wires, 26-gauge for flowers, centers, and leaves; 24-gauge for ring;
    19-gauge for stems

Flower

Cut a 10 or 12" piece of 24-gauge wire and tape it. Coil the piece of wire around a ½" dowel or a straight-sided lipstick case. Remove the wire, and cut it into rings, allowing a ¼" overlap on each one. Tape together the overlap on each ring. *Fig. 78.* Only one ring is used for each daisy, but it is easier to make several than it is to make just one. You will achieve a more perfect circle.

String 45" of beads onto a 55" piece of 26-gauge wire, and crimp one end of the wire to prevent the beads from sliding off. Wrap the open end of the wire around the ring, several times to secure it. *Fig. 79.* Measure 2¼" of beads and form a loop with the beads. Wrap bare beading wire around the ring, at the base of the loop, by pulling the beaded wire around and through the ring. Continue until you have 20 loops. After working 3 or 4 loops, give the wire a double wrap

119

around the ring. This will help to keep the loops more securely in place. At the completion of the 20th loop, weave the remaining bare wire in between and around the base of the first 3 loops, then cut off the excess wire.

Centers

BASIC: 3 beads, round top, round bottom, 12 or 14 rows. Make 1 for each flower.

Because the pattern for the center calls for an even number of rows, you will finish at the top single wire. Allow 3″ of wire, and cut the unit from the spool. Cut open the basic loop at the bottom of the loop. Twelve rows usually covers the center of the flower. If not, make 14 rows.

Leaves

BASIC: 2¼″, pointed tops, round bottoms, 3 rows.
Make 2 for each flower.

Continue for the 4th and 5th rows by making a loopback on the left. This loopback should reach ot the top of the basic row of beads. Wrap beading wire around the bottom of the unit, and repeat this loopback on the right side of the unit, to create rows 6 and 7. Rows 8 and 9 are a shorter loopback on the left. This one should reach to the middle of the basic row of beads. Make a matching loopback on the right for rows 10 and 11. Cut the leaf from the spool, twist the bottom wires together and tape them. Lace the leaf across the center, below the last 2 pairs of loopbacks.

Assembly

Cut a 10″ piece of 19-gauge wire, and cross one end of it over the center of the flower. Bend the wires to the under side of the flower. Twist them together for ½″. Place the center on top of the flower loops and bring the wires of the center together with the stem wires. Twist them together for ½″, and cut off all but the long stem wire. Cover the twisted wires with tape. Put on about 5″ of large green stem beads. Tape the rest of the stem wire, including the last 2 stem beads as you tape. This will prevent the stem from turning. At the base of the stem beads, tape on 2 leaves.

Flower—1¾" wide.

STAR DAISY

The Star Daisy is a good complement to the small California Poppy. They are about the same size, the petals of one are round, and the petals of the other one are pointed. The same leaf count can be used for both.

Materials

Flower, 1 bunch will make 6 flowers
Centers, 1 strand in a contrast color
Leaves, 1 bunch green beads will make 30 to 34 leaves
Wire, 28-gauge for all parts

Petals

BASIC: 10 beads, pointed tops, round bottoms, 5 rows. Make 5 for each flower.

Reduce to 2 the number of wires at the base of each petal by cutting open the basic loop at the base of each petal.

Stamen

Make one 10-bead loop in a contrast color. Make 1 for each flower.

Leaf

BASIC: 10 beads, pointed tops, round bottoms, 7 rows. Make 2 or 3 for each flower.

Assembly

Stack 5 petals, right sides up, bottoms even, and twist the wires together to form a stem. Fan out the petals to form a circle and lift the petals up from the bottom and out at the top to shape the flower. Slide the stamen into the center and wrap the stamen wires around the stem of the flower. Tape the stem. To the flower stem, tape on 2 leaves. Give the leaf a ½" stem. These flowers may be mounted singly or in groups. Use pieces of 16-gauge wire for mounting.

Flower—1¼″ long, 1½″ wide; leaf—2″ long,
1¼″ wide; cluster—5″ high, 4″ wide. See Plate I.

SWEET PEAS

There are 7 flowers and 5 leaves to this cluster of sweet peas (LATHY-
RUS ODORATUS)—an excellent filler for bouquets. Their natural colors
are soft and subtle, and two-toned. The instructions that follow are
for two-colored flowers.

Materials

Flower, approximately 2 strands will make 3 petals
Leaves, ½ bunch
*Wires, 26- or 28-gauge for all parts; 8″ piece of 16-gauge for stem-
    ming*

Petals

Large. The end result of this petal will be two 12-bead loops sur-
rounded by 5 rows of beads (12 rows in all, counting the first loops).
Make a long basic loop with no beads on the top basic wire. Use a
generous amount of wire for the top basic wire (about 6″). *Fig. 80.*
On the left side of the basic wire, form a narrowed, horizontal loop
of 12 beads, starting the loop at the bottom, and bringing it to the
top. *Fig. 81.* Wrap the beading wire around the top basic wire.
Form a second 12-bead loop, narrowed and horizontal, on the right
side of the basic wire, directly opposite the loop on the left. Wrap
the feed wire around the basic loop. Bead around this "frame,"
wrapping the wire, top and bottom, as you work, until there are 6
wraps of beads on each side of the basic wire. There should be 12
rows in all, counting the initial 2 loops. Count the rows directly

122

across the center or up and down; it makes no difference. Trim off the top basic wire, as usual, and cut open the bottom basic loop at the bottom of the loop, leaving 3 wires at the base of the petal. *Fig. 82.* Make 1 in color 1 for each flower.

Small. The small petal is made in the same way, except that the count is altered. Make two 10-bead loops and continue wrapping around them with beads until 10 rows have been completed. Do *not* cut off the top basic wires on the small petal, and leave at least 8″ of bare spool wire at the bottom of the petal before cutting the petal from the spool. Onto this extended piece of bare wire, feed enough beads of color #1 (or a third color) to make a loop of beads that extends from the bottom of the petal, to the top of the petal, and down to the bottom of the petal. Work this loop of beads on the right side of the petal. *Fig. 83.* Twist the bottom wires together to secure the loop, and give the loop of beads 2 half twists. Make 1 in color 2 for each flower.

Assembly of Flower

With the right side of the petals facing you, insert the top basic wire of the small petal into the top of the large petal. The wire should be

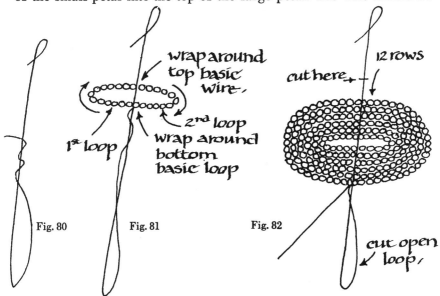

Fig. 80   Fig. 81   Fig. 82

inserted between the last row and the next to last row of the large petal. Bring this wire down the back of the large petal, and twist it in with the bottom wires. Cover these wires with tape. Give the flowers a tight pinch at the basic wire, then bend the outside edges outward.

Leaves

BASIC: 1", pointed tops, round bottoms, 13 rows. Make 5 in green. Work with a generous bottom loop, and cut open the loop at the base of the loop.

Assembly

All flowers and leaves should be taped before combining them to the master stem. Tape the flowers to the top of a piece of 16-gauge wire. Vary the lengths on the flower stems between 3¼ to 2½". Add the leaves, one at a time, at the same place on the master stem. Tape them right side facing the flowers, and allow 1" of stem on each leaf. Bend the top of the heavy stem wire forward, spread out and shape the leaves, and arch the stems of the flowers.

At least 2 colors should be used for the sweet pea flowers, because it is a two-layer flower. Use the predominating color for the small petal, as it sets on top of the larger one, and is, therefore, more obvious. If you make the large petal in pale pink, the small petal in deep pink, you can trim the small petal with a loop of pale pink. If you wish to incorporate a third color, trim the small petal with the pale yellow or red. Sweet peas come in many delightful blends of color from bright fuchsia and white to pale pinks, lavenders, and yellows, and they are lovely in all of them.

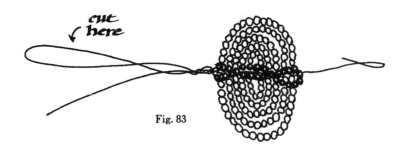

Fig. 83

Flower—1⅛″ wide; cluster—
4¼″ wide including leaves.

SWEET WILLIAM

DIANTHUS BARBATUS is made with a cluster of 20 flowers in each head.
Pink, red, rosy purple, white or varicolored forms are popular.

Materials

Flowers, 10 strands of beads for one head of 20 flowers
Stamens, 1 strand in a contrasting color
Leaves, ½ bunch green beads
Wires, 26- or 28-gauge for flowers, leaves, and stamens.
  16- or 18-gauge for stem

Flower

Four inches from the open end of the spool wire make an oval loop
with 1″ of beads. Repeat for 8 more loops (9 in all) measuring 1″
of beads for each oval loop. Allow 4″ of bare spool wire at the end
of the 9th loop, and cut the flower from the spool. Close the flower
by balancing the wires. To do this, bring the end wire under loop 1
and up between loop 1 and 2. Pull the wire so that loops 1 and 9
are close together, and the loops form a circle. Bring this wire down
between loops 2 and 3, under loop 3, up between loops 3 and 4, and
down between loops 4 and 5. Now the 2 wires are opposite each other
on the under side of the loops. Twist the 2 wires together. Make 20
for each head.

Stamens

Four inches from the open end of the spool wire, make a loop of 5
beads. Wrap around this loop with beads and tightly twist the

wires together, allowing 4″ more of spool wire. Then cut the wire from the spool. Make 1 in a contrasting color for each flower.

Assembly of Flowers and Stamen

Set 1 stamen flat and in the center of each flower. Twist the 2 sets of wires together and cover them with tape that has been cut in half, lengthwise. This will allow the flower stem to remain slim.

Leaves

BASIC: 1″, pointed tops, round bottoms, 13 rows. Make 5 for each 20 flowers.

Work with a long basic loop—about 8″ in all—and cut open the basic loop at the bottom of the loop. Tape the wires.

Assembly of Flowers and Leaves

Cut and tape a piece of 16-gauge wire about 6 or 7 inches in length. Tape all 20 flowers—one at a time—to the top of the 16-gauge wire, allowing 2½″ of stem for each flower. Tape on the leaves, one at a time, all at the same level, around and under the flowers, leaving 1½ to 2″ of stem on each leaf. Continue taping to the bottom of the heavy stem wire. Bend the flower head forward and shape the leaves by coiling them slightly.

```
1          2          3          4          5
|____|____|____|____|____|____|____|____|____|
```

Overall—3½" high, 4" wide; flower—1" wide.

VIOLETS

Bunches of violas make a lovely filler for any bouquet or may be used alone in a small nosegay.

Materials

One 20" strand of beads will make 2 flowers
Six 20" strands of beads will make the leaves and calyx

Flower

(Made with continuous crossover loops.)
Six inches from the open end of the wire, make a narrow loop of 1" of beads. Bring beads up the front and down the back of the loop. This makes one petal. Without cutting the petal from the spool, continue making four more petals in the same manner. Allow 6" of bare wire at the finish of the 5th petal and cut the flower from the spool. Bring the end wire under the first petal, and up between the first and second petals. Put 2 yellow beads onto this wire, cross the wire over the center of the flower, and down between petals 4 and 5. Twist both wires together at the base of the flower for an inch or so. Make 7 or 8.

Bud

The bud consists of one petal of the flower. Make a narrow loop of 1" of beads and give the loop a four-row crossover. Twist the wires together. Make 2 or 3.

Calyx

Make 2 continuous single loops using 10 beads for each loop. Make 1 for each flower and bud, in green.

Leaves

BASIC: ¾" pointed tops, round bottoms, 11 rows. Make 5. Work with a long basic loop—about 8"—as some of it will be used as a stem. Cut open the basic loop at the bottom of the loop.

Assembly of Flowers and Buds

Place the base of each flower in between the two loops of each calyx. Twist together the wires of both the flower and the calyx, then cover the combined wires with tape. Attach a calyx to each flower and each bud and tape the wires.

Assembly of Bunch

Tape the leaf wires. Tape a 6" piece of 16-gauge wire. Attach a piece of tape to the top of the heavy stem wire and tape on all the flowers, one at a time, allowing 2½ to 3" of stem on each flower. The flower stems should be of various lengths. Be sure to add all of the flowers at the same place—the top of the heavy wire. Add the buds a bit lower than the flowers. Add the leaves, one at a time, around the stem, allowing 1" of stem showing on each leaf. Add the leaves right side up. Continue taping to the bottom of the stem wire. Bend the top of the stem wire forward, shape the leaves, and arrange the flowers into a soft cluster.

Flower—5″ wide; leaves—5½″ wide.

WATER LILY

The water lily (NYMPHEA) comes in pink, red, lavender, yellow, blue or white. The centers are usually a pale yellow, no matter what tone is used for the petals. A fairly large flower, use it with other flowers, or arrange 6 or 7 of them by themselves in a low crystal bowl so that they seem to be floating on water.

Materials

Flower and bud, a little more than a bunch
Centers, 2 strands in a contrast color
Leaves, approximately 4 strands for each leaf
Wires, 16-gauge for stemming; 26- or 28-gauge for flowers; 24-gauge for frame of leaf; 30- or 32-gauge for stringing green beads for leaves and beading stems of flowers and leaves

Petals

Unit 1. BASIC: 1″, pointed tops, round bottoms, 9 rows. Make 6 for each flower.

Unit 2. BASIC: 1¼″, round tops, round bottoms, 9 rows. Make 6 for each flower.

Unit 3. BASIC: 1″, round tops, round bottoms, 7 rows. Make 10 for each flower.

Centers

Unit 1. BASIC: 4 beads, round top, round bottom, 8 rows. Make 1 for each flower.

Because this unit has an even number of rows, you will finish at the top of the unit, where the single wire is. Twist these 2 wires together. Open the basic loop at the bottom of the loop, and twist these 2 wires together. Combine all 4 wires together in the center of the wrong side of the unit, and twist them together.

Unit 2. Make 6 continuous single loops, measuring 1½" of beads for each loop. Set Unit 1 in the center of Unit 2, and twist together the wires of both units. Tape the wires.

Make 1 for each flower.

Bud

BASIC: 1", round top, round bottom, 7 rows. Make 1 petal in the color of the petals and 1 in green.

Stack the 2 petals, wrong sides in, so that the bottoms are even. Twist the bottom wires together and tape them. Spiral the 2 petals so that the green one wraps around the flower petal. Tape the bud to the top of a 6" piece of taped 16-gauge wire and bead the stem like flower and leaf.

Leaves

Cut 7 pieces of 24-gauge wire 5" long. Stack the wires so that they are even at the bottom, and tightly twist the wires together for 1". Use

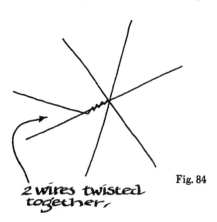

2 wires twisted together.

Fig. 84

2 pliers so that the twisting is tight. Open out the untwisted portion
of the wires to resemble the spokes of a wheel, or the ribs of an umbrella. Twist 2 of the wires together for ¾", measuring from the
center, out. *Fig. 84.* String at least 4 strands of small green beads on
assembly wire. Attach the open end of the spool of assembly wire to
the top of the twisted wires (at the base of the spokes), and wrap it
around the wires several times, tightly. The 2 wires that are twisted
together will be treated as 1 wire until you have worked out to where
it is no longer twisted together. Then you will treat it as 2 ribs. This
will create an open "V" in your leaf. The ribs are going to be treated
as though they are individual basic wires without basic beads on
them. Therefore, you will cross over the top and around each rib as
you work. Start where the 2 ribs are twisted together, by wrapping
the beading wire around it, twice, at the center of the frame. In between each rib put 2 beads—wrapping over and around each rib as
you come to it—until you have 2 beads in between each rib. Work
counter clockwise around the frame. This constitutes the first row.
For the second row, put 3 beads in between each rib, wrapping over
and around each rib as you come to it. Keep the frame flat, and the
ribs as evenly spaced as possible. Continue in the same manner, putting 4 beads in between each rib, for the third row. From here on
the amount of beads need not be counted. Put in whatever amount of
beads it takes to fill the space between each rib. Continue building
the leaf until you have worked 10 rows, counting from the center,
out. This should bring your work to the end—where the 2 ribs are
no longer twisted together. If the wires are twisted beyond this point,
untwist them. If they are not twisted enough, twist them far enough
to accommodate all 10 of the rows. Wrap the beading wire over
and around the right hand wire of the 2 that were twisted together,
then continue putting beads in between each rib, exactly as before,
until you have worked around to the left hand wire of the 2 that
were twisted together. Wrap the beading wire 1½ times around this
rib so that the direction of your work is reversed, then wrap around
to the right side of the leaf, working, this time, from left to right.
When you reach the right hand side again, wrap the beading wire
around the right hand wire 1½ times and again reverse your direc-

tion from right to left. Continue in this manner until you have completed 22 rows of beads. To finish off the beading wire, bring it down the wrong side of the leaf, wrap it around the twisted stem wire several times, and cut the wire from the spool. Trim off the excess 24-gauge frame wires (the ribs) leaving only ¼″ on each one. Turn the ¼″ of wire to the wrong side of the frame, as though it was a top basic wire. Tape the stem. Tape an 8″ piece of 16-gauge wire and tape it firmly to the base of the leaf. This stem may be left plain, or wrapped with small green beads that have been strung on assembly wire. Bead for about 5½″ down the stem, coil the stem around a ½″ dowel for 5½″, leaving 2½″ of stem uncoiled. If a longer stem is needed, mount the leaves on longer pieces of 16-gauge wire. Make at least 2 for each flower.

Assembly of Flower

Tape an 8 or 10″ piece of 16-gauge wire for the stem of each flower. Tape the combined center units directly to the top of the stem wire. Attach a 20″ piece of assembly wire to the base of the center units and wrap it around very tightly, 3 or 4 times. Starting with Unit 3 of the flower petals (the smallest), add them close to the base of the center units, one at a time, wrapping twice, tightly, with each addition. Add the first 5 petals all around, wrong side in, then the next 5 petals in between the first 5, wrong side in. Cup them toward the center units. Add the petals of Unit 2 and then Unit 1 all around the base of the previously attached petals, one at a time, *right* sides up. Thin out the petal wires to 1½″ in length, and cover them with tape. If you are wrapping the stem with small green beads strung on assembly wire, wrap it for about 6″, then coil the beaded part of the stem around a ½″ dowel.

Assembly of Flowers, Bud, and Leaves

Tape together the straight, uncoiled stems of the flowers, bud and leaves. Tape them firmly, as they are heavy. If the stems are beaded, tape together the stems below the beading on the stems.

Head—3½" high
including wire beards.
See also Plate VI.

WHEAT

TRITICUM, a cultivated grass, is shown here with 44 identical units. This form adds height and linear interest to bead bouquets.

Materials

Head, 4 strands butterscotch or gold beads

Wires, 1 small spool 26-gauge brass wire; 1 piece of 16-gauge wire 10 to 14" long

Head

Four inches from the open end of the wire, measure 1" of beads and make a narrow loop of it. Bring beads up the center of the loop, using just enough beads to fit into the center of the loop. Allow 4" of bare wire and cut the wire from the spool. Cross the top wire over the top of the beaded loop, push it through the loop from the back of the loop, to the front of the loop and pull it tight. *Fig. 85.* Make 44.

Assembly

No tape is used to assemble the spike of wheat. Use the gold wire instead. Attach the gold wire to the top of a piece of 16-gauge wire,

133

wrapping it tightly, several times around. Set the base of 1 wheat unit on top of the heavy stem wire and attach it by wrapping the brass wire around, 3 or 4 times, tightly. Work with the brass wire still attached to the spool, as it is difficult to determine just how much you will need. Wrap the brass wire down the stem for ¼", keeping the coils of wire close together. Add 3 more wheat units around the heavy stem, wrap the brass wire down the stem for another ¼ to ⅓" and add 3 more wheat flowers. Wrap twice, tightly, with each addition. Continue on down the stem, adding wheat units as you go, until all 44 have been added. Trim off the bottom excess wheat wires at odd lengths, so that the longest wires are no longer than 2½". Continue wrapping these wires with the brass wire. When they are covered with the brass wire, cut the brass wire from the spool, leaving 4 or 5" only. With this 4 or 5" of wire, wrap up the stem for ¼", and pull tightly so that the wire snaps in between the coiled wire. Repeat once more and cut the piece of wire close to the stem. Cover the remaining part of the stem wire with gold paint so that it will match the brass wire.

Fig. 85

1   2   3   4   5

III *POTTED PLANTS*

Overall—3½" high, 4" wide;
flower—1" wide.
See also Plate XI.

AFRICAN VIOLET PLANT

SAINTPAULIA, — probably America's favorite hobby house plant, with its own society numbering thousands of members,—grows in a variety of colors: shocking pink, pale pink, blue, white, and lavenders and purples.

Materials

Flower, 1 strand will make 2 flowers
Leaves, 20 strands will make all leaves and calyx
Wires, 26- or 28-gauge wire

Flowers

Six inches from the open end of the spool wire, make a narrow loop of 1" beads. Bead up the front and down the back of the loop. This makes one 4 row crossover petal. Without cutting the wire, continue making 4 more petals in the same manner. Allow 6" of spool wire at the completion of the 5th petal, and cut the wire from the spool. Bring the end wire under the first petal, and up between the first and second petal. Put 2 yellow beads onto this wire, cross it over the center of the flower, and bring it down between the fourth and fifth petals. Twist both wires together at the base of the flower for an inch or so. Make 7.

Bud

Execute just one petal of the flower, twist the wires together, and spiral the loop. Make 3.

Calyx

Make 2 continuous single loops using 10 beads for each loop. Make 10 in green, one for each flower and bud.

Leaves

All leaves have pointed tops and round bottoms. There are 5 different sizes. On the large leaves in Units 3, 4, and 5 use a generous basic loop. On all leaves, cut the bottom basic loop wire at the bottom of the loop, so that you finish with 3 wires at the bottom of each.

Unit 1. BASIC: 4 beads, 5 rows. Make 4.

Unit 2. BASIC: 4 beads, 7 rows. Make 4.

Unit 3. BASIC: 6 beads, 9 rows. Make 4.

Unit 4. BASIC: 6 beads, 11 rows. Make 4.

Unit 5. BASIC: 6 beads, 13 rows. Make 8.

Tape all leaves individually.

Assembly of Flower

In between the 2 green loops of a calyx, place the base of a flower. Cup the calyx loops around the flower, twist the wires together then cover the combined wires with tape. Do this to all seven flowers. Attach a calyx to the base of each bud in the same manner, and tape the stems.

Assembly of Plant

Cut a piece of 16-gauge wire the same length as the depth of the container you have chosen for the plant. Tape the wire, and to the top of the heavy piece of stem wire, tape all of the flowers and buds, one at a time. Tape them all around the top of the wire, and all in the same place. Allow 3½" to 4" of stem for each flower and bud. Tape the leaves to the stem wire, one at a time, at the same place as the flowers. Start by leaving ¼" of leaf stems in Units 1 and 2, ½" of stem on the leaves in Units 3 and 4, and ¾" of leaf stem on the leaves in Unit 5. Add the smaller leaves first, then the larger ones. Add the leaves opposite one another. Trim away all wires that are longer than the heavy stem wire, and continue taping to the bottom of the stem wire. The stem will be thick, but none of it will show as the leaves of an African violet plant should grow directly from the soil.

Head—4½" wide.
See also Plate XI.

GERANIUM

PELARGONIUMS are familiar to everyone. Its two most popular colors are, of course, red and pink. However, there is a pure white hybrid with pale green centers that is most attractive. If you are making red or pink ones, work the center in the same color as the flowers.

Materials

Flowers, each flower head of 22 flowerettes requires 1½ bunches

Leaves, 1 bunch green for 1 flower stem

Wires, 28-gauge for flowers and leaves; 16-gauge for master stem

Flowers

Move 8 beads to within 4″ of the open end of the spool wire, and form a loop with the 8 beads. Twist the bottom wires together, twice only, at the base of the loop. Encircle this 8-bead loop with beads, wrap spool wire around the bottom wire once, then encircle the double loop once more with beads, wrapping the spool wire around the other wire once, close to the base of the loops. Make another 8-bead loop ¼″ away from the first petal and wrap this loop, twice, with beads. Continue in this manner until you have made 4 petals in all. Allow 4″ of bare spool wire at the completion of the fourth petal, and cut the flower from the spool. *Fig. 86.* Make 22 for each head.

Centers

Make one 8-bead loop, and allow 4″ of wire for the stem. *Fig. 87.* Insert a center into each flower, twist the wires together to form a stem, and cup the petals of the flowers. Cover the stem wires with floral tape that has been cut in half lengthwise. This will keep the stems slim. Make 1 for each flower.

Leaves (in 2 sizes)

The basic count for both size leaves is 8 beads. Work with a long basic loop and a long top basic wire. Work the leaf through the 10th row, then cut open the basic loop at the bottom of the loop. *Fig. 88.* Spread the 2 bottom wires to form a "V." Treat both wires like basic wires, starting with the 11th row. Bring the beaded wire down for the 11th row and wrap the beading wire around the basic wire on the right side. Wrap 1½ times. The extra half wrap will reverse your direction so that the 12th row will be made as you go back up to the top of the leaf. Wrap around the top basic wire. Come down the left side of the leaf, for the 13th row, wrap the beading wire around the left bottom wire one and a half times. This extra half wrap will reverse your direction so that the 14th row will be made as you go back up to the top of the leaf. Continue with this pattern until you have 18 rows for the small leaf, and 22 for the large leaf. You will finish at the top of the leaf for both sizes. Allow 6 or 7″ of bare spool wire when the leaf is finished, and cut the wire from the spool. Twist together the two top wires and cover them with tape. To the 2 bottom wires, feed on enough small green beads to cover the "V" in the leaf (7 or 8). Push the wires through to the back of the leaf, at the narrow part of the split V. Bring the taped wires down the wrong side of the leaf and twist the two basic wires to it. Tape all the wires. If you have worked with a long enough basic loop and top basic wire, these combined wires will be long enough for the stem of the leaf. Lace the leaves across the center for extra firmness. Make 2 small and 3 large for each head of flowers.

Assembly

Cut and tape 16-gauge wire to the desired length. One piece for each flower head will be sufficient. Leave 2½″ of stem on each flower and tape the flowers, one at a time around the top of the heavy stem wire. Tape them all at the same level. When all 22 of the flowers have been attached, tape down the stem for 1½″ and add the leaves one at a time. Space them 1½″ apart. Add a large one first, then alternate the sizes as you add them. Cut flower stems to desired lengths and pot the geraniums.

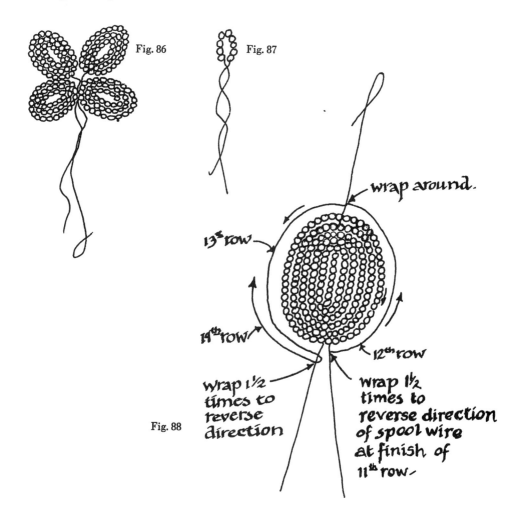

Fig. 86

Fig. 87

wrap around.

13ᵗ row

14ᵗʰ row

12ᵗʰ row

wrap 1½ times to reverse direction

wrap 1½ times to reverse direction of spool wire at finish of 11ᵗʰ row

Fig. 88

Flower—1½″ wide; head—6″ long,
3″ wide. See also Plate XI.

HYACINTH

Hyacinths normally grow in pink, lavender, blue and white. They can be used as an individual potted plant or in large arrangements of cut flowers in the same way you would use lilacs, delphiniums, snapdragons or stock. There are 44 flowers and 5 leaves in the potted plant.

Materials

Flowers, 3½ bunches
Wires, 26- or 28-gauge for flowers and leaves; 16-gauge for stems

Flower

Three inches from the open end of the wire, make a narrow loop of 1½″ of beads. Give this loop a three-row crossover by beading up the front of the loop, and bringing bare wire down the back of the loop. Wrap the wires together twice, close to the base of the loop. Directly next to the first loop, make another loop of 1½″ of beads, bead up the front of the loop, bring bare wire down the back of the loop, and wrap the spool wire around the base of this second loop. Continue in this manner until you have 6 continuous three-row crossover loops. Each crossover loop constitutes one petal. Allow 3″ of spool wire and cut the flower from the spool. Bring the finish wire under the first petal, and up between the first and second petals. Onto this wire put two yellow beads. Cross the wire over the center of the flower and bring the wire down between petals four and five. Twist the two wires together to form a stem. This will lock in the two yellow beads. Tape the stems of each flower, individually. Make 44 flowers for each head.

Leaves

BASIC: 3¼", pointed tops, round bottoms, 7 rows. Make 5.

Assembly

Bend the heads of all the flowers forward before you start the assembly. Cut 2 pieces of 16-gauge wire in proportion to the container. Wire should be 2½ times height of pot; (make a 10" stem for a pot 4" high). Tape both wires individually, then tape them together. Attach a piece of tape to he top of the master stem wire. Tape a flower to the top of it allowing ½" of stem on the flower. Tape down the master stem for ½" and add 2 more flowers, one at a time. Continue taping all of the flowers down and around the stem until all of the 44 have been added. The flower head should measure approximately 7½" when completed. Add the leaves, one at a time, around the master stem wire about 2½" below the last row of flowers. When potted, the leaves should be flush with the top of the container. There should be no stem showing on the leaf itself. Arrange the flowers so that there are no bare spaces between them. Bow out the leaves at the bottom, and in, at the base of the flowers. If the flowers are to be used in an arrangement with other flowers, leaves need not be added.

ORANGE TREE
See Plate XI.

CITRUS SINENSIS is a true conversation piece. It stands nearly 15″ high and measures 9 to 10″ across. To make it a lemon tree, merely use yellow beads and oval cork balls.

Materials

Leaves, 10 bunches green beads

Oranges, 1 bunch orange beads; 10 cork balls ½″ in diameter; glue; small paint brush

Trunk, 1 bunch brown beads

Wires, 26- or 28-gauge for leaves; 22- or 24-gauge for orange stems; four 16-gauge wires for trunk; 18-gauge for stemming of leaves; 30- or 32-gauge for brown beads

Leaves

BASIC: 7 beads, pointed tops, round bottoms, 11 rows. Make 105 leaves, 21 branches of 5 leaves each.

Cut 21 pieces of 18- or 19-gauge wire 9″ long and tape them. Tape the 105 leaves individually. To each 9″ piece of 18-gauge wire, tape 5 leaves—one at the end, and the others space about 1″ apart down the stem. Let ½″ of leaf stem show. *Fig. 89.*

Oranges

For each orange, combine 2 strands of orange beads by tying them together and putting a knot at both ends. Saturate the knot at one end with glue and insert it into the hole of the cork ball. Do this to all of the corks. Make 8 or 10. The glue on the ones you do first will be dry enough for you to work on, by the time you have finished all of them.

Stem

BASIC: 2 beads, round top and bottom, 3 rows. Make 1 for each orange, in green.

Combine the top basic wire and the bottom basic wires in the middle of the wrong side of the tiny round unit, and twist the wires together. Cut a 3″ piece of 22- or 24-gauge wire for each orange stem and bend one end of it to make a ½" hook. *Fig. 90.* Catch the hook into the wires of the underside of the tiny green unit and secure it by taping. Tape several times around so that when you insert the stem of the unit into the glued opening of the cork ball, it will fit snugly. Pull the stem all the way through so that the tiny green unit covers the hole in the cork ball. With a small paintbrush, cover the cork ball with glue and wrap orange beads completely around the cork. By stemming the cork first, then beading the ball, you can turn the cork more easily while you are gluing. Keep the beads and the rows of beads close together as you glue. When the cork has been completely wrapped with beads, cut off any excess, but have a little extra string to tuck into the bottom hole of the cork and fasten with a drop of glue. Add the oranges to the desired branches after the tree has been assembled.

Assembly of Tree

Cut 4 pieces of 16-gauge wire, 15" long. Tape them individually, stack them and tape them together. Around the top of these wires, tape 4 branches of leaves, 1 at a time. Set the branches low, so that the heavy stem wires are just below the bottom leaf of the branch. Tape down the heavy stem wires for 1" and add 4 more branches around the "trunk" of the tree. Continue in this manner until all 21 branches have been added. Continue taping to the bottom of the trunk. String 7 or 8 strands of brown beads on 30- or 32-gauge assembly wire. Wrap the open end of the assembly wire several times, very tightly, around the "trunk" of the tree at the base of the bottom branches. Wrap the trunk of the tree with the brown beads. Shape the branches downward like an umbrella until you have a "ball" of green leaves. Be sure to have the right sides of the leaves on the outside. Attach the oranges to the desired branches by wrapping the orange stems to the branches.

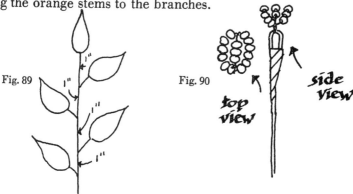

Fig. 89   Fig. 90   top view   side view

Flower—3″ long, 2¼″ wide.

PANSY PLANT

The petals of VIOLA may be shaded individually or may be in contrast colors, large ones in lavender, small ones in yellow, and lip petal in lavender, as one example. Plant the flower stems close together in the center of your container, mount the leaves on an inch or two of heavy stem wire and insert them into the container close to the base of the stems of the flowers. Alternate them so that one curves up and the other curves out and down. Two or 3 flowers, 2 buds and 6 to 8 leaves makes a nice arrangement in a small saucer-shaped container.

Materials

Petals, ½ bunch beads in color
Leaves and Calyx, ½ bunch of green beads
Wires, 28-gauge for flowers; 26-gauge for leaves; 18-gauge for stems

Flower

Large petals. BASIC: 3 beads, round tops, pointed bottoms, 9 rows. Make 2 for each flower.

Small petals. BASIC: 3 beads, round tops, pointed bottoms, 7 rows. Make 2 for each flower.

Lip petal. Make two 8-bead narrowed, horizontal loops on each side of the basic. Wrap around these loops 3 times. This will give the petal 4 rows on each side of the basic. (See Lady Slipper, Sweet Peas for detailed instructions.) Make 1 for each flower.

Calyx

Make 5 continuous single loops counting 10 beads for each loop. Working backwards, make one 20-bead loop at the base of each previously made 10-bead loop. *Fig. 91.* Make 1 for each flower and 1 for each bud, in green.

Bud

Use four-row crossover method. Make a narrow loop of 20 beads, bead up the front and down the back of the loop of beads. Give the crossover loop a half twist in the middle, twist the bottom wires together, and tape them. Tape the base of the bud to the top of a taped 5″ piece of 18-gauge wire. Wrap a calyx around the bud, long loops covering the bud, by looping one calyx wire through the last small loop of the calyx. Pull closed, twist the 2 calyx wires together, and cut them off close.

Assembly of Flower

Make 2 pairs of petals by combining 1 small petal to 1 large petal, even at the bottom. Twist wires together. Place the 2 pairs together, face to face, bottoms even, twist the wires together, and open them. Tape the lip petal to the 2 pairs by placing it right side in, and even at the bottom. When it is securely taped, bend the lip petal forward and down. Make a stamen by forming a loop with 10 beads. Slide

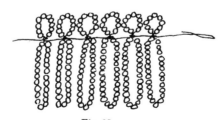

Fig. 91

this 10-bead loop into the center of the flower. Tape the base of the flower to the top of a 7½″ piece of taped 18-gauge wire. Add a calyx in the same way as for the bud. However, have the smaller loops at the base of the flower.

Leaf

Basic: 1½″, round top, pointed bottom, 9 rows.

When the above count has been completed, continue by adding 2 loopbacks on each side of this section. Make the first loopback on the left and have it reach to the middle of the basic. Make the second loopback on the right and the same height as the first loop. The third and fourth loopbacks—one on the left and one on the right—should reach to the bottom of the basic. Open the basic loop at the bottom of the loop. Tape the wires, and reinforce the stems with a 2″ piece of taped 16-gauge wire.

Overall—17½" high; flower—8" wide.
See also Plate IX, XI.

SUNFLOWER

HELIANTHUS, the sunflower, is perfectly named, as it is truly the sunniest flower of them all, and must, of course, be made in yellow. The flower is big and bold, measuring over 7" across, and it is important enough to stand alone. Plate XI shows it in a velvet pot made with velvet tubing that has been glued to an ordinary 3 by 5" clay pot filled with modeling clay.

Materials

Flowers, 4½ bunches yellow beads
Center Units, ½ bunch black or dark brown
Leaves and Calyx, 1 bunch green beads
Wires, three 16-gauge or two 14-gauge for stems; 28- or 26-gauge for flowers and leaves; 30- or 32-gauge for assembling and beading the stem

Petals

Unit 1. BASIC: 1½", pointed tops, round bottoms, 7 rows. Make 15. Reduce to 2 the number of wires at the bottom of all petals by cutting open the basic loop at the base of the petals.

Unit 2. BASIC: 2½", pointed tops, round bottoms, 9 rows. Make 18 for each flower.

Reduce the number of bottom wires to 2.

Centers

Unit 1. BASIC: 6 beads, round top, round bottom, 12 rows. Make 1 in black or dark brown for each flower.

Make this unit round and flat. Finish the 12th row at the top, twist the spool of wire to the top basic wire, cut open the basic loop at the bottom of the loop. Join both sets of wires together in the middle of the wrong side of the unit and twist them together. *Fig. 92.*

Unit 2. Make 12 continuous single loops measuring 2½" of beads for each loop. Insert Unit 1 in the center of Unit 2 and twist both sets of wires together. Make 1 for each flower.

Unit 3. Make 14 continuous single loops, measuring 3¼" of beads for each loop. Place Units 1 and 2 into the center of Unit 3 and twist all wires together. Cover the wires with tape. Make 1 for each flower.

Calyx in Green Beads

BASIC: 12 beads, round tops, very pointed bottoms, 9 rows. Make 5 for each flower.

Leaves

Small. BASIC: 1", pointed tops, round bottoms, 7 rows. Make 2.

Medium. BASIC: 1¼", pointed tops, round bottoms, 7 rows. Make 4.

Large. BASIC: 1½", pointed tops, round bottoms, 9 rows. Make 4.

Reduce to 2 the number of wires at the base of each leaf by cutting open the loop at the base of the leaf, and cover them with tape.

Assembly of Flower

Cut either 2 pieces of 14-gauge wire or 3 pieces of 16-gauge wire about 14" long. Tape the wires individually—3 if they are 16-gauge; 2 if they are 14-gauge—then tape the wires together, side by side.

The flower is heavy. If you wish, you can use wire hangers cut to the required lengths and tape them together.

To the top of the taped stem wires, tape the combined center units. At the base of the center units wrap, very tightly, a 20"-piece of assembly wire (30- or 32-gauge wire). With the assembly wire, add the small petals around the base of the center units. Add them, one at a time, wrapping twice tightly, right sides up, with the assembly wire. After adding 7 or 8 petals, wrap a layer of tape close to the base of the flower. This will prevent the assembly wire and the petals themselves from slipping as you assemble. When all of the small petals have been added, add the larger ones in the same manner, adding more assembly wire as needed. Wrap another layer of tape every now and then, as needed. When all petals have been added, thin out the petal wires, cutting them at uneven lengths, then cover them with tape. Lace the calyx leaves together—as for tulip petals —starting at the base of the basic row. *Fig. 93.* Lace with the right side of the leaves facing you. When all rows have been laced, fold the

Fig. 92

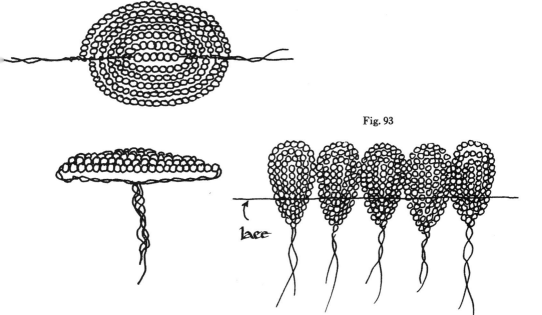

Fig. 93

lace

5 leaves in half—wrong side in—twist the lacing wires together and cut away all but ¼". Tuck to the wrong side the ¼" of twisted lacing wire.

Insert the stem of the flowers into the top of the laced calyx leaves. Push the calyx up to the base of the flower and tape the calyx wires to the stem wire.

Combine the leaves as in *Fig. 94*. Make 2 groups of leaves using 1 small, 2 medium, and 2 large leaves for each group, combining them like a palm. Tape a pair of medium leaves ½" down the stem of a small leaf. Tape a pair of large leaves ½" down the stem of the 3 combined leaves.

Tape one group of 5 leaves on the left side of the master stem, 5" below the base of the flower. Tape the second group of 5 leaves 2" below the first group, but on the right side of the master stem. Bend the head of the flower forward. The stem should be wrapped with small green beads strung on assembly wire. Wrap the stem all the way down to the point where it enters the pot.

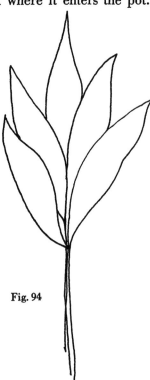

Fig. 94

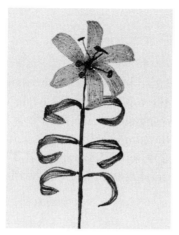

Overall—14" high; flower—4" wide.
See also Plate XI.

TIGER LILY

TIGRIDIAS are bold and graceful. Their petals can be turned back with a downward curve to allow the stamens to stand out prominently, or they can have a tighter, bell-like appearance. To emulate Nature, you can choose yellow and orange ones, or the dotted kinds—yellow with light brown dots, orange with dark brown, and white and pink ones dotted with ruby red. Most varieties have brown centers. A potted plant of 2 or 3 flowers is a show piece. Extra leaves at the bottom of the long-stemmed flowers make the effect even more realistic. (See Plate XI.)

Materials

Flowers, 1½ strands beads for each petal
Stamens, 1 strand beads in contrast color
Leaves, 2 bunches green beads
Wires, 26-gauge on all parts; 16-gauge for stems

Petals

BASIC: 2", pointed tops, round bottoms, 13 rows. Make 6 for each flower.

Stamens

BASIC: 2 beads, round tops, round bottoms, 5 rows. Make 6 in a contrasting color for each flower.

Work with a long basic loop. Open the basic loop at the base of the stamen. Combine the top and bottom basic wires of each stamen in the middle of the wrong side. Give the wires 3 tight twists. Cut off all but 1 wire. Onto the single wire that is left, string green beads. Put 2″ on 2 stamens, 2½″ on 2 stamens, and 3″ on 2 stamens. Twist together all 6 wires at the base of the green beads.

Leaves

Small. BASIC: 3½″, pointed tops, round bottoms, 7 rows. Make at least 6 for each flower stem if the flowers are to be treated as a potted plant. If they are to be used in an arrangement with other flowers, 4 leaves may be sufficient, depending on the height and the surrounding flowers.
Large. BASIC: 4″, pointed tops, round bottoms, 9 rows. Make 12 to 20 for the base of the potted plant.

Bud

Make 1 extra flower petal, in color, for each bud, then execute the same size petal in green, for each bud. Stack 1 on top of the other, wrong sides in, and twist the wires together. Cut off all but 2″ of the wires and tape them to a 6″ piece of taped 16-gauge wire. Spiral the petal and the leaf tightly, so that the green leaf wraps around the petal. Make 1 or 2.

Assembly of Flowers

Combine the flowers by stacking all 6 petals, one on top of the other, right side up, bottoms even. Twist the bottom wires together tightly, and cover the wires with tape. Swing the petals into a circle. Lift the petals up from the bottom and bend them out at the top. Slide the combined 6 stamens in between 2 of the petals so that the green beads are at the bottom of the flower petals. Tape the flower stems and the stamens together.

Thread a large embroidery needle with about 10″ of 30- or 32-gauge wire, and sew the 6 petals all around the outside, about one-third of the way up from the bottom of the flower. Stitch the basic row and the first and last row of each petal. Draw the petals together with the wire, so that the flower is firm. The petals will overlap slightly. When all of the petals have been sewn, remove the needle, twist the lacing wires together, cut off all but ¼″ of the wire and tuck the remaining ¼″ of wire inside the flower.

Assembly of Flowers and Leaves

Tape all leaf wires. This is a heavy flower; therefore, use two 16-gauge wires, taped singly and then tape together, for each flower. Cut different lengths for each flower, and cut before taping as it is easier to cut bare single wires. Use a heavy duty cutter, not the same one you are using for the beading wire. Continued use on heavy wire will dull a small cutter, and even nick it beyond repair.

To the top of a double 16-gauge wire, tape a flower, very firmly. Place the top of the stem wire very close to the base of the flower. Tape on pairs of leaves approximately 2″ apart down the stem. Bend the head of the flower forward, and curve the leaves up and out.

For a potted plant, tape on 2″ pieces of 16-gauge wire to the base of each large leaf, and insert the leaves into the container at the base of the flower stems, all the way around the container. Insert the bud stems into the container directly next to the flower stems or tape them to the flower stems before potting.

IV MINIATURES

Flower—1¼" wide.
See also Plate X.

APPLE BLOSSOM

The apple blossoms' true colors are pale pink with deeper pink centers, or white with pale yellow or pale pink centers. Either combination is lovely. The branch shown here in black and white, and the one in Plate X is made with pale pink petals. The centers are in deep pink edged in white. The flowers can be used as branches or grouped in clusters.

Materials

Flower petals, 12½" of beads for each
Centers, 10 dark pink beads plus 1" of white
Leaf, 7½" of green beads for each
Wire, 28-gauge for stringing; 18-gauge for branches

Flower

Four inches from the crimped end of the wire, make an oval loop of 15 beads. Twist the wires together, twice, at the base of the loop. Encircle the 15 bead loop with a row of beads, and twist the wires together, twice, at the bottom of the loop. Directly next to the first loop, make another 15 bead loop, twist the wires together, and encircle the second loop with a row of beads. Wrap the spool wire around the base of the second loop to secure the wrapped around row of beads. Continue in this manner until 3 more petals have been completed. Tightly twist the two wires together at the base of the flower to form a stem.

Leaves

BASIC: 10 beads, pointed tops, round bottoms, 7 rows. Make 1 or 2 for each flower and tape the stems.

Centers

Make one for each flower.

Make a loop of 10 beads. Allow 5″ of bare spool wire at the end of the loop and cut the wire from the spool. Onto this wire, feed enough beads in a contrast color to encircle the 10 bead loop. Twist the wires together. Set one center in the middle of each flower so that it is flat. Twist the 2 sets of wires together and tape them. Cup the petals slightly.

Assembly for Branch

Tape a 10 or 12 inch piece of 16 gauge wire. To the top of the heavy wire, tape a leaf, then a flower, then two leaves, then two flowers, then a leaf, etc., until the desired length has been achieved. Space the flowers and leaves about ½″ apart. Leave ½″ of stem showing on each flower, and ¼″ of stem on each leaf.

Assembly for Cluster

To the top of a short piece of taped 16 gauge wire, tape 4 or 5 flowers, allowing 2½ to 3 inches of stem on each flower. Tape 5 or 6 leaves at the same place on the 16 gauge wire, allowing ½″ of stem for each leaf, then continue taping the remaining part of the 16 gauge wire all the way to the bottom. One or two clusters make a charming filling for a small cup and saucer.

MINIATURE BUDS
Flower—½" high, ¾" wide.
See also Plate X.

Materials

Buds, 2 strands beads in color
Leaves, calyx and ferns, 3 strands green beads
Wire, 26-gauge brass

Buds

Three inches from the open end of the spool wire, make a beaded loop, measuring 1" of beads for the loop. Narrow the loop and give it a 4-row crossover by beading up the front and down the back of the loop. Twist the wires together for ½". Leave 3" of bare spool wire, and cut the bud from the spool. Give the bud a twist so as to make it spiral in appearance. Make 15.

Calyx

Three inches from the open end of the spool wire make two 10"-bead loops. Twist the wires together, twice, at the base of the loops. Leave 3" of wire and cut the calyx from the spool. Make 15 in green.

Combining Bud and Calyx

Set the base of the bud between the 2 green calyx loops. Twist the wires of both units, tightly, to form a stem.

Leaves

Make a narrow loop of 3" of beads. Give this loop a 4-row crossover, by beading up the front and down the back of the loop. You need only 2" of wire for stems. Make 5.

Curly Fern

Three inches from the open end of the spool wire, make a 10-bead loop. Twist the 2 wires together for ¼". On the left side of the wire, make another 10-bead loop. Directly opposite this loop, make another 10-bead loop. Twist the wires together for ¼", on the left side of the wire, make another 10-bead loop, directly opposite this loop, make another 10-bead loop. Continue in this manner until you have made 4 pairs of loops, topped by the first loop. Twist the wires together at the bottom. *Fig. 95.* Make 5 or 7 in green.

Assembly of Bud Cluster

Cut a small piece of 16-gauge wire the length of the depth of the container to be used, and tape it. To the top of this wire, tape all the buds. Vary the lengths of the bud stems from 2¼" to 1½". Add the leaves—no stems showing—in the same place as the buds on the stem wire. Add the curly fern around the stem. Cut off any wires that are longer than the heavy stem wire and cover all wires with tape.

Fig. 95

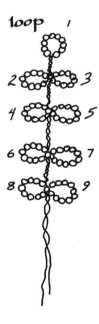

Sprig (left)—2½″ wide; flower—½″ wide.
Cluster (right)—2″ wide;
flower—½″ wide.

FORGET-ME-NOTS

MYOSOTIS (Greek for mouse ear) is the correct botanical description for this appealing garden subject, mainly blue-, pink-, or white-flowered in nature.

Forget-me-nots can be combined in clusters of 10 or 12 flowers with 5 or 6 leaves, or in sprigs using 2 or 3 small leaves, 5 or 6 flowers and 2 or 3 large leaves.

Materials

Flowers, 40 beads for each flower
Leaf, small leaf—approximately 27 beads; large leaf—approximately 60 beads
Wires, 26-gauge brass or 28-gauge silver

Flower

Make 4 continuous single loops, using 10 beads for each loop. Then twist the wires together. When making flowers for a sprig, leave 4″ of wire at each end of the 4 loops. *Fig. 96.* For a cluster, 2″ is sufficient.

A 2-bead center (in contrast color) may be added if desired. (See Queen Anne's Lace.)

Leaves

All leaves have pointed tops and round bottoms.

Small. BASIC: 5 beads, 3 rows.
Large. BASIC: 5 beads, 5 rows.

Cut open the basic loop at the base of the loop, as all 3 wires are needed for firm stems.

Assembly of Clusters

Tape a 2″ piece of 16-gauge wire and tape 10 or 12 flowers to the top of it, one at a time, leaving about 1½″ of stem on each flower. Add leaves one at a time. Trim off all brass wires at the bottom of the 16-gauge wire and cover the end with tape.

Assembly of Sprig

Build a sprig of flowers by starting it with 1 small leaf. Twist the stem of 1 flower to the stem of the small leaf, allowing ⅓″ of stem for each. Add another small leaf and 2 flowers ⅓″ further down the stem, continuing until the desired length has been achieved. Tape a short piece of 16-gauge wire to the bottom of the sprig. *Fig. 97.*

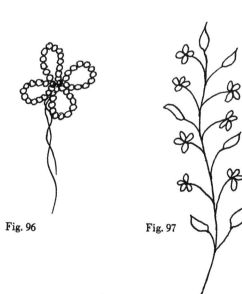

Fig. 96   Fig. 97

Flower—1" high; leaf—1½"
long. See also Plate X.

MINIATURE IRIS

This tiny iris is made in 2 parts. Both parts are made in the same way, and both parts can be made in the same color. However, they are prettier if 2 colors are used.

Materials

Flowers, ½ strand of beads for each flower
Leaf 5" green beads for each leaf
Wire, 26-gauge brass

Petals

Five inches from the open end of the spool wire, make a narrow loop with 1" of beads. Bead up the front of the loop, cross over the top of the loop and bring bare wire down the back of the loop. This makes a 3-row crossover petal. Twist the wires at the base of the crossover loop twice, tightly, close to the base of the loop. Close to this first crossover loop, measure another 1" of beads, make a narrow loop of it, bead up the front of this second loop, and bring bare wire down the back of the loop; wrap spool wire around base of second loop. Continue until you have made 1 more 3-row crossover loop close to the second one. Allow 5" of bare spool wire at the end of the 3rd loop and cut the unit from the spool. Repeat for the other half of the flower, either in the same color, or in a contrast color. It takes

2 of these units to make a flower. Combine these 2 units by setting one on top of the other. For the top unit, place the wrong side up, so that the bare wires show. Set the other unit under the top one, right side up. Arrange the petals so that they alternate—right side up, then wrong side up, then right side up, etc. Keep the units flat and twist the stem wires together tightly. Cup the petals of the top unit up and in, so that the wire side is inside. Bend the bottom unit petals downward. *Fig. 98.*

Leaves

BASIC: 1¼", pointed tops, round bottoms, 5 rows. Make 2 for each flower.

Cut the bottom basic loop at the bottom of the loop, and twist the wires together.

Assembly of Iris

Make a grouping of 3 iris and 6 leaves, by taping them all, one at a time, to the top of a taped piece of 16-gauge wire. Vary the lengths of the stems on the flowers, but not the leaves.

Fig. 98

Flower—½″ high, ¾″ wide.
See also miniature daffodils in Plate X.

MINIATURE JONQUIL

These tiny jonquils—members of the NARCISSUS family—can be made in one solid color, two shades of yellow or yellow and white. Those shown have pale yellow crowns and deeper yellow petals. Leave long wires on all flower units, as these will form the stems. If brass wire is used, the stems need not be taped. If silver wire is used, cut the floral tape in half, lengthwise, and then tape. This will keep the stems slimmer and in proportion to the size of the flowers.

Materials

Flowers, 1 strand for each flower
Leaves, 7″ strand green for each leaf
Wires, 26-gauge brass or 28-gauge silver; 16-gauge for reinforcing
   stems

Petals

BASIC: 7 beads, pointed tops, round bottoms, 3 rows. Make 6 for each flower.

Reduce to 2 the number of wires at the bottom of each petal, by cutting open the basic loop at the base of the petal.

Crown

Make 8 continuous single loops, measuring 1″ of beads for each loop. Close the loops by twisting the end wires together. Bell out at the bottom of the crown, and give the tops of the loops a sharp bend outward to give a fluted effect. Make 1 for each flower.

Assembly of Flowers

Stack the 6 petals one on top of the other, right side up, and twist the wires together to form a stem. Open the petals to form a circle of petals, and set the bottom of the crown onto the 6 petals by sliding the crown wires in between 2 petals. Combine all wires, and twist for the full length of the wires. To shape, bend the petals up from the bottom and down at the tip so that they arch slightly. Tip the head of the flower forward from the base of the flower.

Leaves

BASIC: 1¼", pointed tops, round bottoms, 5 rows. Make 2 for each flower.

Reduce to 2 the number of wires at the base of all leaves. Attach 2 leaves to each flower stem by wrapping the leaf stems around the flower stems 1½" below the base of the flower. To the top of a short piece of taped 16-gauge wire, tape 4 or 5 flowers together to form a cluster.

MINIATURE PRIMROSE
See Plate X.

Primulas are low-growing perennials. Make 3 flowers for a front view arrangement, and 4 or 6 for an all-around arrangement. The flowers can be worked in 2 colors (layered) or in 1 shade. The following instructions are for 2 colors.

Flower

Unit 1. Make 3 continuous single loops using 8 beads for each loop. Do not twist the wires. Make 1 in color 1 for each flower.

Unit 2. Make a loop of 8 beads, and encircle the loop with beads (wraparound). Continue on the same wire by making another 8-bead loop, encircle it with beads, then make a third loop of 8 beads and encircle it with beads. (See Wraparound Method in General Instructions chapter.) Do not twist the wires together. Make 1 in color 2 for each flower.

Unit 3. Make this unit in the same manner as Unit 2 but increase the number of beads on the loops to 10. Do not twist the wires together. Make 1 in color 1 for each flower.

Assembly of Flower

Set Unit 1 on top of Unit 2. Twist the stem wires 2 or 3 times to hold them together. Set the combined Units 1 and 2 on top of Unit 3 and twist all the wires together, tightly. The tighter the twist, the neater and firmer the stem, when you are working with brass wire. Crush the loops upward to form a ball.

Bud (in either color)

Make 3 or 6. Make a narrow loop of 1″ of beads and give the loop a 4-row crossover by beading up the front and down the back of the loop. To the base of the bud, add a calyx of 2 ten-bead loops made in green. Twist the 4 wires together tightly, to form a stem.

Curly Fern

Four inches from the open end of the spool wire, make a loop of 10 beads. Twist the wires together for ¼″. On the left side of the wire, make another 10-bead loop and twist it closed. Directly opposite this loop, make another 10-bead loop and twist it closed. Twist the wires together for another ¼″ and make another pair of 10-bead loops the same way. Continue in this manner until you have completed 4 pairs of loops. Twist the bottom wires together. These curly ferns can be made all in green, or some in green and some in the color of the flower. Make 5 or 7. Open the loops to round circle by inserting a pencil, large nail, or orange stick into each circle.

Assembly of Primrose Cluster

Tape a short piece of 16- or 18-gauge wire no longer than the depth of the container that is to be used. Tape all the flowers, buds, and ferns to the top of it, one at a time, leaving no more than 1½″ of stem showing on the tallest flower, and 1″ on the remaining ones. Cut off all brass wires that extend below the heavy stem wire and cover the bottom of the wire with tape. Photo consists of 3 flowers, 3 buds, and 5 curly ferns.

Flower—1¼" high, 1" wide; cluster—4" high.
See also Plate X.

MINIATURE TEA ROSES

These most elegant members of the ROSA family are good in flower arrangements and delightful as potted plants.

Materials

Petals, 4 or 5 strands beads for the flowers
Leaves, 3 or 4 strands green beads
Baby breath, 1 strand white beads
Wire, 26-gauge brass

Petals

All petals are round, top and bottom. Work with a long basic loop, and cut the loop open at bottom. These wires will be the rose stems. Twist the bottom wires of the petals only once.

Large. BASIC: 5 beads, 9 rows, Make 2 for each flower.

Small. BASIC: 5 beads, 7 rows. Make 2 for each flower.

Assembly of Flower

Cup, wrong side in, the 2 small petals, and entwine them so that the petals form an overlap on each side. (See Large Rose.) Twist the wires together for ¼". Add the 2 large petals, right side in, one at a time, at each overlap of the combined 2 small petals. Twist all

165

bottom wires together, tightly, to form the stem of the rose. Bend out the tops of the large petals to shape.

Leaves

BASIC: 5 beads, pointed tops, round bottoms, 5 rows. Make 3 for each rose and each rose bud.

Work with a long basic loop. When the leaf is finished, cut open the basic loop at the bottom of the loop, leaving 3 wires on each leaf. Twist the wires together and combine the leaves as in *Fig. 99*. Attach the leaves to the rose stems by wrapping the leaf wires around the rose stems.

Buds

The bud is the rose without the 2 large petals. Combine the 2 small petals, as for the rose, twist the wires all the way to the bottom, and add a sprig of 3 leaves to the stem. Make 3 or 4.

Baby's Breath

Make 2 or 3 sprigs, using the brass wire. (See Baby's Breath.)

Assembly of Rose Cluster

Tape a piece of 16- or 18-gauge wire no longer than the depth of the container that is to be used. To the top of this heavy wire, tape all flowers, buds, and Baby's Breath, varying the lengths of the stems on all. The tallest rose should be no higher than 1½ times the height of the container. Trim off all excess brass wire at the bottom of the heavy stem wire, and cover the bottom of the wire with tape. Photo shows 8 roses, 4 buds, 10 curly fern and 3 baby breath.

Fig. 99

MINIATURE TRITOMA

The tritoma (KNIPHOFIA) is more effective if it is done in 3 shades of beads, using the palest shade at the top, and graduating to the deepest shade at the bottom.

Materials

Flowers, 3 colors, a few strands of each
Leaf, 12" green beads for each leaf
Wire, 26- or 28-gauge for flower and leaf; 16-gauge for stem

Flowers

Unit 1. 5 continuous single loops measuring 1¼" of beads for each loop. Make 1 in color 1.

Unit 2. 6 continuous single loops measuring 1⅓" of beads for each loop. Make 2 in color 2.

Unit 3. 7 continuous single loops measuring 1½" of beads for each loop. Make 2 or 3 in color 3.

Assembly of Flowers

Close all loop units by twisting their wires together. Tape an 8" piece of 16-gauge wire for the stem. Insert the stem wire into Unit 1, leaving only ¼" of the stem wire inside the loops of Unit 1. Tape the wires of Unit 1 for ½" and cut off the remaining wires. Insert the bottom end of the stem into one Unit 2. Have the top of Unit 2 reach the middle of the loops of Unit 1. Tape the wires of the unit to the master stem for ½" and cut off the remaining wires. Insert the stem into the second Unit 2. Have the top of this unit reach the middle of the preceding one. Tape the wires to the master stem for ½" and cut off the remaining wires. Continue in this manner until all of the units have been added. Three inches below the bottom unit, tape on 2 leaves.

Leaves

Make a narrow loop of 6" of beads. Give this loop a 4-row crossover by beading up the front and down the back of the loop. Tape the stem wires. Make 2 for each flower.

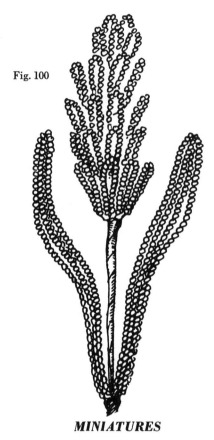

Fig. 100

MINIATURES

My purpose in designing miniatures was threefold. First, it is an excellent way to use the small amounts of leftover beads. Second, miniatures can be executed quickly—buds and primrose clusters, for example, can be completed in less than two hours. And last, tiny arrangements are a delightful "bread and butter" gift, especially if the colors are selected to harmonize with the decor in the home of the hostess. However, these are not for the beginner, as the brass wire is soft and the component parts are very small. Work on larger flowers first to familiarize yourself with the directions of the wire and get the "feel" of the materials involved. The use of gilded brass wire makes stem-taping unnecessary. Therefore, stems are kept slim and well-proportioned to the blossoms.

V HOLIDAY AND TABLE DECORATIONS

4" high, 3" wide at base.
See also Plate XII.

CHRISTMAS ANGEL

The angel is made with two identical parts which are joined when completed.

Materials

½ bunch gold or silver bugle beads
1 large crystal bead for the head
26- or 28-gauge wire

Part 1

String at least 3 strands of beads before starting. Both parts are continuous loops, so do not cut the wire from the spool until Part 1 is completed. Starting with the wings, 10" from the open end of the spool wire, make a wide, pear-shaped loop with 2¾" of beads. Bead up the front and down the back of the loop, giving it a 4-row crossover. Next to it make another wide loop with 2¼" of beads, bead up the front and down the back of the loop. Make another wide loop with 1¾" of beads, and bead up the front and down the back of the loop. These three 4-row crossover loops constitute one set of wings (1 large, 1 medium, and 1 small). Without cutting the wire from the spool, create the first section of the gown by making three continuous loops, measuring 6" of beads for each loop. Make the loops close together at the base. Continue on the same wire, and create one arm by making a narrow loop, measuring 3" of beads for the loop. Give this loop a four-row crossover by beading up the front and then down the back of the loop. Continue on the same wire, and create another section of the gown by making 3 continuous single loops, measuring 6″ of beads for each loop. Allow 4″ of bare spool wire at the completion of the last loop, and cut the wire from the spool. *Fig. 101.*

Part 2

String at least 3 more strands of beads and repeat the above pattern. Combine the 2 parts by joining the gown wires, so that the wings are at opposite ends. *Fig. 101.*

Skip lace the gown loops ⅓ of the way down from the top. Pull the gown loops close together. Be careful not to include the arms. Point them up, and out of the way. When the skip lacing is finished, fold the 2 parts in half, twist together the lacing wires and cut off all but ½″. Tuck in the ½″ of twisted wires. Twist together the wires at the base of the 2 large wings. Gather all 4 wires (2 from the gown and 2 from the wings), and twist them together for ¾″. Cut off all but the longest wire. Cover the twisted wires with white floral tape. Onto the long wire, put the large crystal bead for the head. Push it down onto the taped wires, as far as it will go. To create the halo, string 25 bugle beads onto the long wire. Make a ring out of the last 20 beads by wrapping the wire between the 5th and 6th beads several times. Cut off the excess wire very close to the beads. Bend the arms down, and shape the gown into a bell. If you wish to hang your angel on a Christmas Tree, tie a narrow satin ribbon around its neck.

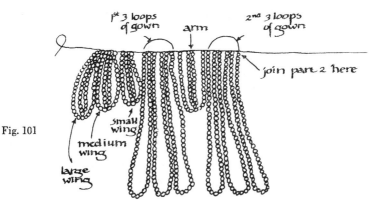

Fig. 101

Overall—6″ high; small bell—1″ high, 1¼″ wide; medium bell—
1¼″ high, 1½″ wide; large bell—1½″ high, 2″ wide.
See also Plate XII.

CHRISTMAS BELLS

These little bells need not be confined to Christmas. One or two of them nestled into the center of a large satin bow make an elegant trimming for an anniversary or wedding present.

Materials

Bells, 8 strands beads
Wire, 26- or 28-gauge

Bells

Large. Make 20 continuous single loops, measuring 3″ of beads for each loop. Keep the loops very close together at the bottom. Make 1.

Medium. Make 16 continuous single loops, measuring 2½″ of beads for each loop. Keep the loops very close together at the bottom. Make 1.

Small. Make 14 continuous single loops, measuring 2″ of beads for each loop. Keep the loops very close together at the bottom. Make 1.

Before closing each bell, skip lace them ⅓ of the way down from the top, then fold them in half—wrong sides in—twist the lacing wires together for ¼″, cut off all but the ¼″ of twisted wires, and tuck them inside the bells. Combine the beginning and ending wires by twisting them together only twice. Center these wires by bringing one of the wires to the opposite side of the circle of loops. Hook it through the base of the middle loop, then bring both wires to the center of the circle and twist them together.

Clapper

Four inches from the open end of he spool wire, make a loop using 1" of beads. Give the loop a 4-row crossover by beading up the front of the loop, and down the back. Allow 4" of bare wire and cut the clapper from the spool. Twist together, twice, the wires at the base of the loops.

Small. Feed one inch of beads onto each wire, then twist the wires together. Make 1 for each bell.

Medium. Feed 1¼" of beads onto both wires. Make 1 for each bell.

Large. Feed on 1½" of beads onto each wire. *Fig. 102.* Make 1 for each bell.

Into each bell, insert the right sized clapper, and join the clapper wires and bell wires together by twisting them at the top of each bell. A large gold bead may also be used as a clapper.

Make 5 continuous single loops, measuring 1½" of beads for each loop. Make one of these for the top of each bell to cover the opening at the tops of the bells. Add them as you would a calyx to a bell flower. Gather together all the bell wires, twist the ends together, wrap them with satin or velvet ribbon, and add ribbon bow.

Fig. 102

17" high. 7" wide at base.
See also Plate XII.

CHRISTMAS TREE

A brilliantly beaded tree shimmering with sequins of red, gold, blue, silver and green will provide holiday glamour for years to come, as this is truly an heirloom piece. It is 15 glittering inches tall and can be made in either gold, silver or green beads. There are 35 branches to the tree. Some are larger than others, but the technique is the same for all. Use a small ruler for measuring; your work will go faster.

Materials

3 bunches beads for branches
Sequins for tree decoration
14- or 16-gauge wire for stem
3 strands beads for festoons
26- or 28-gauge wire for stringing
1 spool of fine wire for attaching sequins (32- or 34-gauge)

Branches

Three inches from the open end of the spool wire, measure 1¼″ of beads and make a loop with them. Twist the wire tightly, twice, at the base of the loop. Push 7 beads to the base of the loop, and adjoining this, make another loop of 1¼″ of beads and twist the wires together, twice, at the base of the second loop. If you are making a gold or silver tree with bugle beads, put only 4 beads between the loops, as these beads are longer. Continue in this manner until you have made 5 loops in all, separated by 7 beads. *Fig. 103.* Keep the loops oval in shape. Allow 3″ of bare wire at the end of the 5th loop and cut the branch from he spool. Make 4 more branches exactly the same way.

Using the same technique as before, make 4 branches with 7 loops, 4 branches with 9 loops, 6 branches with 11 loops, 6 branches with 13 loops, 6 branches with 15 loops, and 4 branches with 17 loops. Fold each branch in half, *Fig. 104,* and make a half twist in between each pair of loops. *Fig. 105.* Twist the two bottom wires together, and cover the wires with tape.

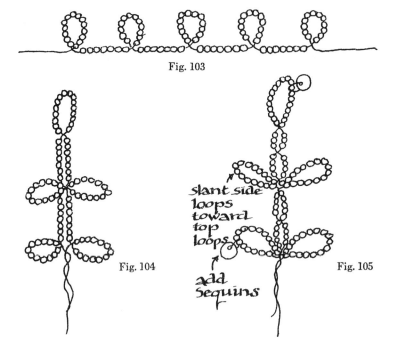

Fig. 103

slant side
loops
toward
top
loops

add
sequins

Fig. 104

Fig. 105

Trimming the Tree

Cut short pieces of assembly wire—about 1½"—insert one piece into the hole of each spangle or sequin, twist the wires together, and hook the spangles onto the branches of the tree. Use 2 for each small branch, 3 or 4 for the larger ones.

Assembly of Tree

Cut 2 pieces of 16-gauge wire 15" long. Tape them individually, then tape them together for extra firmness. Starting with the smallest branches and gradually using the larger ones, tape the branches to the heavy stem wire, one at a time, and all around. Each set of branches should be approximately ¾" apart as you add them down the stem. If you want a truly glamorous pot, choose one that measures 3" high and 3" in diameter, and cover it with glitter.

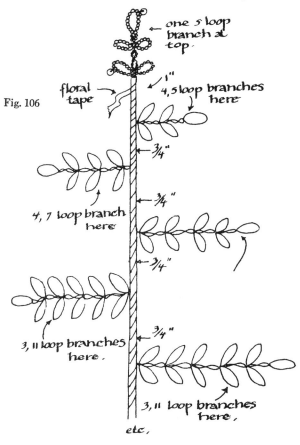

Fig. 106

Overall (life size)—12" high,
5¾" wide. See also Plate XII.

POINSETTIA

The poinsettia (pronounce poin-set i a) is the most traditional of all holiday plants, with its bright red petals adding a colorful touch to any room. The count for 3 sizes has been included in the pattern. Make a life-size plant for a real conversation piece for your buffet table, a medium-sized one for cocktail table, or a small one for giving.

Materials

Flowers, 3 bunches red beads
Stamen, 2 strands yellow beads
Leaves, 1½ to 2 bunches green beads
Wires, 26- or 28-gauge for all parts; 16-gauge for stems

Petals For Life Size Plant

Large. Basic: 1¼", pointed tops and bottoms, 9 rows. Make 5.
Small. Basic: 1", pointed tops and bottoms, 7 rows. Make 5.

Petals For Medium Size Plant

Large. Basic: 1", pointed tops and bottoms. 7 rows. Make 5.
Small. Basic: ¾", pointed tops and bottoms, 7 rows. Make 5.

Petals For Small Size Plant

Large. Basic: ¾", pointed tops and bottoms, 7 rows. Make 5.

Small. Basic: ½", pointed tops and bottoms, 5 rows. Make 5. Reduce to 2 the number of wires at the base of each petal by cutting open the basic loop at the base of the petals.

Stamens

For large and medium flowers. Basic: 3 beads, round tops, round bottoms, 6 rows. Make 3 in yellow for each flower.

For small flower. Basic: 3 beads, round tops, round bottoms, 4 rows. Make 3 in yellow for each flower.

Cut open the basic loop at the bottom of the loop. Because the stamen has an even number of rows, you will finish at the top of the stamen. Twist both sets of wires together, then join both pairs of wires in the center, on the wrong side of the stamen, and twist them together. Cut floral tape in half, lengthwise, and tape all flower petals and stamens.

Leaves

Large. Basic: 1½", pointed tops, round bottoms, 11 rows. Make 6 for each large flower stem.

Execute the first 9 rows as you would for any other leaf. The 10th and 11th rows are going to have loops added to them. One-third of the way up the 10th row, make a 15-bead loop, two-thirds of the way up the 10th row make another 15 bead loop, and finish off the 10th row. On the 11th row, work down one-third of the way and make a 15-bead loop. Work down another third of the way, and make another 15-bead loop. Finish off the 11th row. Twist the bottom wires together, cut open the basic loop at the bottom of the loop and tape the stem. *Fig. 107.*

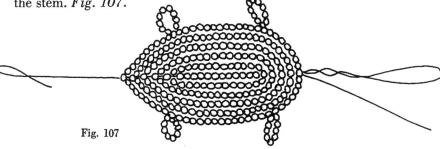

Fig. 107

Medium. BASIC: 1¼″, pointed tops, round bottoms, 9 rows. Make 5 or 6 for each medium flower stem.

Make these leaves in the same way, but add two 12-bead loops on the 8th row and 9th row.

Small. BASIC: 1″, pointed tops, round bottoms, 7 rows. Make 4 for each small flower stem.

Make these leaves in the same way, but add two 10-bead loops on the 6th row and the 7th row.

Stemming Flower and Leaves

Use two 16-gauge wires taped together, for the stem of the large flowers. Single 16-gauge wires are strong enough for the medium and small flowers. The assembly is the same for all flowers.

To the top of a stem wire, tape 3 stamens. Allow ½″ of stems on the stamens. Attach a 15″ piece of assembly wire ¼″ below the top of the stem wire. Secure it by wrapping it 3 or 4 times. Add 5 small petals, one at a time, around the stamens. Allow ½″ of stem on each petal. Wrap tightly with the assembly wire, as each petal is attached. Add the large petals around the small petals, one at a time, wrapping twice, tightly, with the assembly wire. Thin out some of the petal wires by cutting them off at uneven lengths. Cover the remaining wires with tape. About 2″ below the base of the flower, tape on a pair of leaves—opposite one another. Another 2″ below the first pair, tape on a second pair opposite one another, etc., until the required number of leaves have been added. Bend the head of the flower forward. Cut the stems to the desired length.

For a life-size plant of poinsettias, combine 2 large flowers and 1 medium flower. For a medium size plant, pot 2 or 3 medium flowers. For a small plant, pot 2 or 3 small flowers.

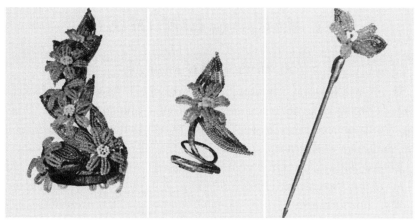

Candle bobêche—6″ high, 3″ wide; place card holder—2¼″ high, 2¾″ wide; canapé pick—3½″ high including pick, 1½″ wide. See also Plate I.

TABLE ACCESSORIES

Many items other than flower bouquets can be made with beaded flowers. For example, in the table setting color plate there is a pair of candle *bobêche* and place card holders. In the close-up black and white photograph, a canapé pick has been added to the grouping.

The place card holder is made from a 12″ piece of 16-gauge wire. Tape a small flower and a pair of small leaves to the top of the wire. You may merely cover the whole 12″ of wire with tape or you can use metallic thread or narrow satin ribbon for covering. If you use thread or ribbon, start with glue and finish with glue at the end so that the thread or ribbon won't unravel. The stem can be wrapped with small green beads strung on assembly wire too. After the stem is covered with the material of your choice, coil the wire around a ⅝″ dowel, then shape the coils so as to balance the flowers. Insert a name card in between the coils of wire behind the flower.

The candle *bobêche* is made with a taped piece of 16-gauge wire 30″ long. To make the frame, coil the taped wire around a dowel or straight-sided glass bottle 1¾″ in diameter. Extend one end of the coil, 3½″ of it, to form the top of the *bobêche*. Tape together the remaining coiled wire to form a ring. This is the base that will rest on the rim of your candlestick. To the top of the frame, tape leaves and flowers, alternately, down the single wire and around the coiled base. It takes about 14 leaves and 9 flowers to cover the frame. You can use a small three row crossover daisy, an apple blossom, a star daisy, or any delicate flower.

179

VI *MAKING BOUQUETS*

FLOWERS AND LEAVES

1. If you are making a bouquet of assorted bead flowers and foliage, include some spike forms, some round ones, and some fillers. Trailing plants or sprays of flowers or leaves allowed to flow down from the container add grace.

Round flowers used for center of interest or dominant focus are anemone, carnation, chrysanthemum, daisy, daffodil, dahlia, day lily, morning glory, rose, oriental poppy, etc. Clusters of opened small flowers such as the geranium, sweet William, and Queen Anne's lace can also be used as dominant flowers.

Spikes are used to give height, line, and accent and to form the basic pattern. Use delphinium, gladioli, forsythia, etc.

Airy small flowers are used as fillers: viola, phlox, babies'-breath, etc. Some of these smaller flowers if grouped and flattened can be used as focal flowers. Leaves are also used as fillers.

2. Flowers look best if they are set at different heights. Do not hesitate to cut down the stem, using *heavy* snips. Also add to the stem if necessary. One good way is with a wire coat hanger cut the desired length and secured to a beaded stem with floral tape. The taping should not be allowed to show in the finished design.

3. If you are using only one kind of flower, show it in different stages of growth—bud, partly open, fully open. The full-blown mature flowers should be assembled so that they are lowest on the stem, used at the center of interest. You can easily simulate different stages of growth by flattening the flower to open it or compressing it to close it, or by reducing the number of petals.

4. Give depth to your bouquet by facing the flowers and leaves in varied directions—left, right, and front. If you are making a free-standing arrangement, you will also have to complete the back by filling it in.

5. Assemble the bead flowers and leaves so that the materials with the least weight, color strength, and size are at the outside boundaries of the design, on the tallest stems. Use your most important, most colorful, most compelling flowers at the center of interest on the shortest stems. The center of interest is usually the place where the vertical stems of the beaded flowers or leaves cross the horizontal

lines of the container at the point of insertion.

6. Group and tape your bead flowers and leaves whenever possible, following the design pointers given above, and noting the information given later in this chapter under *Details of Plates*. When materials are grouped, you have fewer stems to insert and the design seems to flow from a common source, which is desirable in making flower arrangements.

CONTAINERS

1. Select a container which harmonizes in color with the beaded flowers. If the container has painted decorations, unity is achieved if the bead flowers echo the painted decorations in color and in form. Inexpensive containers can be spray-painted to blend with the bead colors.

2. The size of the container is a matter of judgment. For a mass bouquet, try a container about one third the size of the finished bouquet. That is, if you are planning a bouquet to stand 15" high, your container should be about 5" high. The same proportions apply with horizontal designs. However, if your bouquet is open and airy —a line arrangement rather than a mass arrangement—the container can be considerably smaller and still be in good proportion.

3. Pack non-hardening floral clay into the container of your choice about two thirds of the way to the top and around the sides. Now make a mound of clay in the center, rounding it so that it does not touch the sides. All flower sprays will be inserted into this mound of clay so that they will appear to be growing from one root or trunk, just as they would in nature. You may need as much as ten pounds of clay or as little as two pounds for this. Be careful with delicate containers that you do not force the clay or pack it in too hard. Try to work the clay in your hands first or warm it in the sun or slow oven. Conceal the mound of clay with sheet moss available at florists'.

Tall containers. Cardboard tubes from paper towels are a great help when potting an arrangement in a tall vase. Fill the tubes with clay, then set them into the vase. If the tall vase is transparent, cover the cardboard tube with glue, roll it in florist sheet moss, then insert it in the vase. Should the tube need to be secured and balanced, anchor a pinholder at the bottom of the vase with a small amount of clay or Permagum, insert the tube firmly, then wrap a coil of clay around the top of the tube at the top opening of the vase, pressing the clay to the outside edge of the vase so as to make the tube steady. Use the size tube that best fills the inside of the vase, pressing the clay to the outside edge of the vase to make the tube steady. Cover top with moss. Obtain tubes used for yard goods. They are longer and can be cut to size with a sharp knife.

Silver containers. If you choose a bowl which will need polishing, try to find an inexpensive glass or plastic container (plastic can be cut down if the sides are too high) to use as a liner. The flowers and the liner can then be easily removed when the silver needs to be polished.

Cut-glass containers. Any transparent container needs a liner to conceal the clay. Fill the bowl with clay, leaving an inch of space between the clay and the inside of the bowl. This space can then be filled with moss, and the clay won't show through the glass bowl. Cover the top of the clay with more moss. Liners can also be made from double thicknesses of heavy aluminum foil, which can be lifted out without disturbing the flowers; however, a small amount of clay should be placed in the bottom of the bowl first to hold the foil liner firmly in place.

COLOR

Most people who are interested in making bead flowers seem so sophisticated in their use of color as to make this section perhaps unnecessary. Still, some pointers about developing a color plan might be helpful.

1. Inspiration for color schemes can come from many sources. Your garden border with its tulips, irises, and jonquils could be the beginning of a lovely spring bouquet. Of if you have developed a room

scheme you like or have found a painting or fabric which is *dernier cri* as far as you are concerned, you can't go wrong if you copy its color in beads. Just use the same intensities and the same proportions in your bouquets.

2. Use the strongest, brightest, most intense color at the center of interest. You can repeat this color throughout the design, but in smaller amounts (a small bud at the tip could repeat the big splash of color in the dominant flower or flowers).

3. Don't fight your center of interest. Your biggest, roundest flower or flowers should be made in the most attention-getting color combinations so they compel the eye.

4. For the sake of color balance, use your weakest colors at the tips, away from the fulcrum or center-of-interest area, just as in a seesaw the light child moves to the edge to balance the heavy child close to the center.

5. Pale beads seen in the light or with light shimmering behind them become even paler, but pale beads used as the center of interest, in shadow and against foliage, look darker. Therefore, even if you are making a bouquet of only one color (besides the foliage, of course) your arrangement will have color contrast.

6. White does not count as a color, but it's marvelous for giving a lift to almost any scheme. Be sure to echo the white beads by using them rhythmically (not spottily) throughout the design, maybe in the container too.

7. How to work out a color scheme from a color wheel:

Complementary. Select opposites on the color wheel, for example, violet and yellow.

Split complementary. Instead of direct opposites, use the hues on either side, for example, violet with yellow-green and yellow-orange.

Analogous. Any three colors lying next to each other on the color wheel, for example, red-violet, red, and red-orange.

Monochrome. Any one color, but used with lots of different shapes and with many different values of the same hue, for example, pale pink, shading to light violet to purple (see Plate I).

Triads. Any of three colors equidistant on the color wheel, for example, yellow, red, and blue.

8. It is an accepted fact that colors create definite effects on people, definite moods, too. Some schemes stimulate, others relax. Bold reds, oranges, and yellows are warm and full of vitality—good in modern, informal, and cheerful settings. These are the colors often associated with autumn. Tudor and Jacobean period styles use rich combinations of these colors.

Blues and greens are cool and restful, reminding one of water and remote sky. A color scheme of blues, greens, and yellow-greens will give a feeling of early spring. Sheraton's favorite color was blue, which he used with lots of white and also with yellow.

Pastels are feminine, often used in bedrooms which are personal rooms. French court styles used pale tints and soft pastels with lots of white and gold accents.

Dark tones are somber, could be depressing, but are also heavy and rich. Victorians used them with lots of dark gold.

DESIGNS AND PATTERNS

It will help you in making your flower arrangement to think of a design pattern before you actually make your bouquet. Select a pattern from the following group, keeping in mind the number of beaded flowers you have to work with and the place where the bouquet is to be used.

A mass arrangement is one which has a more or less compact or closed form. It includes focal flowers, fillers, and material used for line. Even when making an arrangement of this type, do not crowd the blossoms together; give each one room to breathe. Plate V is an example of a mass arrangement.

A tall vertical is best against a tall narrow background; a wide horizontal design is best on a dining table. If you have very few bead flowers, a line arrangement is to be preferred to a mass. Once you gain confidence from using these traditional designs, there is no reason why you cannot go on to making modern compositions in

free-form patterns of your own choosing. The most popular basic
designs are illustrated here:

SIX STEPS IN MAKING AN ASYMMETRICAL TRIANGLE DESIGN

Plate VII can be used as your guide. Pack your container with clay and cover it with sphagnum moss as described earlier in this section under "Containers."

1. Group your spike materials so that the smallest, palest buds are highest on the stem. This will help you achieve balance in your design. Select a grouping of spike forms which is about twice the height of the container you are using, exclusive of that portion of the stem which will be concealed in the clay. The concealed portion should be almost equal to the depth of the container, since all bead materials should be inserted as deep into the clay as possible. (All measurements are variable: heavy groupings can be only one and one-half times the height of the container, etc. Consider these measurements as suggestions, not as rules.) Insert this first grouping in the back center of the mound of clay. Make certain that the tip is straight up from the stem, not tilted.

2. Select another group of spike forms which is two thirds the height of the first one. Insert it directly in back of the first group, but curve it towards the right.

3. Select another group of spike forms which is one third the height of the first one. These can be larger forms than in the first groupings, or can be opened somewhat to seem larger. Insert this group directly in front of the first group, but curve it towards the left. You have now established the height and width of your design.

4. Assemble your flowers so that the largest ones are lowest on the spray, and the buds at the top. The largest ones can be shown full face. The intermediate flowers can be shown turned, some to the left, some to the right. Recess one or two flowers to give depth and add variety to the design. The buds should be at the top: each bud and flower should be at a different height. Give each one room to "breathe."

5. Place this grouping of flowers in front of the spike forms. Bend the wires as necessary to make certain that each one is at a different level, facing different directions. One or two flowers may be drawn

down to partly conceal the opening. If you wish, bend one flower down below the opening; bend another one so that it is half above and half below the opening; this will give transition to your design 6. Insert any leaves you are using as filler materials if your design requires it.

CARE OF BEAD FLOWER BOUQUETS

Your beaded flowers are completely washable. Remove the flowers from the container, fill a large bowl with lukewarm water and add to it a capful of liquid soap, not detergent. Swish each flower in the solution, then rinse in clear cool water. Set the flowers on paper or Turkish towels to dry, then rearrange them in their container. Before removing the flowers, you might like to draw a diagram showing the location of each flower in the bouquet. This will make rearranging easier, and you will have a better chance of putting it back together again as it was originally. On the other hand, this might be the time to try a new design!

If the arrangement you wish to wash is a small one, it is not always necessary to remove the flowers. Cover the container with aluminum foil or Saran Wrap to keep it watertight, turn the container upside down and swish the flowers first in the soapy solution, then in clear cool water. Return the container to an upright position to dry, then unwrap the container.

Bead flowers never become tiresome, for they sparkle and gleam as though full of motion when seen through light. Still there is no reason to stick to only one design. Don't be timid about dismantling the bouquet; this is part of the fun! You can achieve so many different effects with the same bead flowers and leaves. Gently pull out the stems from the clay, then scoop out the clay with a spoon. If the clay has hardened, soften it in the sun or in a warm oven. The clay can be used again—and, of course, the bead flowers will last forever! The many arrangements shown can be used as inspiration for your own designs or can be copied exactly. If you wish to copy one, choose your favorite and build it up following the basic instructions given earlier in this chapter. A list of the materials follows for each plate.

DETAILS OF PLATES

Inside Back Cover

I PINK AND WHITE TABLE SETTING, 17″ high. 1 cluster morning glories, pink with white edges; 4 clusters sweet peas in pink and white; 4 clusters white lady's slippers with pink centers and 7 leaves to each cluster; 10 pink daisies with deep pink centers, two leaves to each. 2 candle *bobêche* each made with 9 daisies and 16 leaves. 4 placecard holders, each with 1 daisy and 2 leaves. Gold and white compote.

Inside Front Cover

II TULIP IN A FOOTED MESH CONTAINER, 18½″ high. Eighteen tulips on 12″ pieces of 16-gauge wire, stems wrap-beaded for 9″. Six groups of tulips, 3 to a group, assembled by taping unbeaded portions of stems together. Four leaves added at bases of beaded stems. Fern and ivy leaves for fillers.

III FORSYTHIA, JAPANESE LANDSCAPE STYLE, 24″ high. Four groupings of forsythia, each one containing 4 twigs of varied lengths, assembled into one trunk. Gold metal bowl, with rocks as accessories.

Page 3

IV A SYMMETRICAL TRIANGLE IN BLUES AND WHITE, 21″ high. Three fantasias, one aqua edged in teal blue, 2 white edged in aqua; 3 rose of sharon in teal with white center (single, 3 leaves each); 6 rose of sharon in white with aqua center, 2 pairs on 1 wire, 3 leaves each; 2 singles, 2 leaves each. Daisies: 26 in white with aqua center. 3 groups of 4 daisies, 5 leaves each; 4 groups of 3 daisies, 3 leaves each; 1 group of 2 daisies, 2 leaves each. Aqua glass container.

V A HORIZONTAL MASS BOUQUET, 26″ wide. Delphiniums: 2 full length, 2 half length (minus 5 large flowers at the bottom); 4 lavendar lilacs, 1 pink lilac; 6 pink carnations; 7 pink anemones with lavender centers; 1 pink and purple fuchsia. Purple glass compote.

Front Cover

VI GROUPING OF AUTUMN FLOWERS, Orange Container, 18″ high: 4 orange oriental poppies, 2 yellow oriental poppies; 4 butterscotch wheat; 2 half sprigs of Chinese lanterns, 3 flowers each. White container, 5½″ high: 4 yellow marigolds, 4 leaves each; 5 orange marigolds, 4 leaves each. Dahlia: 1 orange and yellow, 3 leaves.

Inside Back Cover

VII ASYMMETRICAL TRIANGLE OF DAFFODILS AND PUSSY WILLOWS, 33″ high. Pussy willows: Tallest grouping consisting of 9 twigs in various lengths; second grouping, 4 twigs in varied lengths; third grouping, 2 twigs, varied lengths; short twig of two used in front as filler. Daffodils: nine, two leaves each, assembled on a single stem. Largest flowers at center of interest. Others facing different directions.

Back Cover

VIII THREE INFORMAL BOUQUETS. Anemones, 11″ high: An all-around arrangement in a blue and white bowl with 44 anemones, 3 leaves each. Rose spray in red bud vase: 23½″ high: 1 bud with 3 leaves, 1 medium rose with 3 leaves, 1 large rose with 3 sprigs, 5 leaves each; all material on one stem. Lenox China Swan, 16″ wide: 6 large sprigs of baby's breath; 4 sprays of roses (1 bud, 1 medium and 1 large rose to each spray, 3 leaves to each flower); 18 buds, 3 leaves each; 4 medium roses, 3 leaves each; 2 large roses, 5 leaves each.

Page 4

IX THREE BOUQUETS IN VARIED HEIGHTS. Lenox China Vase; 40″ high: 14 chrysanthemums in white, yellow and orange; 10 gladioluses in white and yellow; 1 cluster of 3 white rose of sharon. Wicker basket, 16½″ high: 10 short sprigs of forsythias, 5 on each side; 5 day lilies, 2 groups of sunflower leaves as fillers. Brass cornucopia, 11″ high: 3 clusters of morning glories, 3 flowers and 9 leaves to each cluster.

Page 5

X MINIATURES. Left to right, heights are listed: Tea roses and baby's breath, 8″; shasta daisy, 9″; buds in swan, 3″; irises, 5″; daffodils, 5″; apple blossoms, 11½″. In front are tea roses in compote, 4″; primroses, 3″ in egg, 2″ in gold box.

XI POTTED PLANTS. Left to right: Sunflower, 18″; Orange Tree, 18″; African violet, 6¼″; Cabbage Rose, 18″; Hyacinth, 11½″; Tiger Lily, 19½″; Geranium, 16″.

Page 6

XII CHRISTMAS DECORATIONS. Left to right: Silver tree, 17″; Green Tree, 19″; Small Poinsettia plant, 9½″; Angel, 4″; bells, 6″ circumference.

INDEX